Python Programming

This Book Includes:

Python Programming For Beginners + Tips And Tricks + Data Science

Learn Computer Languages in One Day Effectively (#2020 Version)

Steve Tudor

Legal & Disclaimer

The information contained in this book and its contents is not designed to replace or take the place of any form of medical or professional advice; and is not meant to replace the need for independent medical, financial, legal or other professional advice or services, as may be required. The content and information in this book has been provided for educational and entertainment purposes only.

The content and information contained in this book has been compiled from sources deemed reliable, and it is accurate to the best of the Author's knowledge, information and belief. However, the Author cannot guarantee its accuracy and validity and cannot be held liable for any errors and/or omissions. Further, changes are periodically made to this book as and when needed. Where appropriate and/or necessary, you must consult a professional (including but not limited to your doctor, attorney, financial advisor or such other professional advisor) before using any of the suggested remedies, techniques, or information in this book.

Upon using the contents and information contained in this book, you agree to hold harmless the Author from and against any damages, costs, and expenses, including any legal fees potentially resulting from the application of any of the information provided by this book. This disclaimer applies to any loss, damages or injury caused by the use and application, whether directly or indirectly, of any advice or information presented, whether for breach of contract, tort, negligence, personal injury, criminal intent, or under any other cause of action.

You agree to accept all risks of using the information presented inside this book.

You agree that by continuing to read this book, where appropriate and/or necessary, you shall consult a professional (including but not limited to your doctor, attorney, or financial advisor or such other advisor as needed) before using any of the suggested remedies, techniques, or information in this book.

Table of Contents

PYTHON PROGRAMMING

The Practical Beginner's Guide to Learn Python Programming in One Day Step-by-Step (#2020 Updated Version | Effective Computer Programming)

Steve Tudor

CHAPTER 1. WHAT IS PYTHON

Python is basically an incredibly useful and powerful language. It's present essentially everywhere. Everything from the scripting side of video games (or the video games themselves) to intensive server-side web applications to the plethora of deep and responsive desktop applications that have been built with it.

When should you use Python? The answer depends upon exactly what you're going to do. But since you're a beginner, I say you should learn anyway.

As you continue to grow as a programmer after this book, you're going to learn when you should and shouldn't use Python just as a matter of intuition. Python is an absolutely fantastic language, but the place where it fails is when you have to get extremely close to a computer's hardware or write incredibly efficient programs. In these areas, Python doesn't excel.

However, that's not to say it doesn't have its perks. In fact, I'd say that's one of the few places that Python falls flat. And what it lacks there, it makes up for in other areas. For example, development time in Python is generally extremely low in comparison to other languages. This is super easy to illustrate. Compare the following excerpts of code, the first from C++, the second from Java, and the last from Python.

A. WHY TO LEARN PYTHON

Learning the ABCs of anything in this world, is a must. Knowing the essentials is winning half the battle before you get started. It's easier to proceed when you are equipped with the fundamentals of what you are working on.

In the same manner that before you embark on the other aspects of python let us level off the basic elements first. You need to learn and understand the basics of python as a foundation in advancing to the more complicated components. This fundamental information will greatly help you as you go on and make the learning experience easier and enjoyable.

Familiarize yourself with the Python Official Website https://www.python.org/. Knowing well the website of python would give you the leverage in acquiring more information and scaling up your knowledge about python. Also, you can get the needed links for your work

Learn from Python collections. Locate python collections such as records, books, papers, files, documentations and archives and learn from it. You can pick up a number of lessons from these, and expand your knowledge about Python. There are also tutorials, communities and forums at your disposal.

Possess the SEO Basics. Acquire some education on Search Engine Optimization so you can interact with experts in the field and improve your python level of knowledge. That being said, here are the basic elements of Python.

B. DIFFERENT VERSIONS OF PYTHON

With Guido van Rossum at the helm of affairs, Python has witness three versions over the years since its conception in the '80s. These versions represent the growth, development, and evolution of the scripting language over time, and cannot be done without in telling the history of Python.

The Versions of Python Include The Following;

- **Python 0.9.0:**

The first-ever version of Python released following its implementation and in-house releases at the Centrum Wiskunde and Informatica (CWI) between the years 1989 and 1990, was tagged version 0.9.0. This early version which was released on alt.sources had features such as exception handling, functions, and classes with inheritance, as well as the core data types of list, str, dict, among others in its development. The first release came with a module system obtained from Module-3, which Van Rossum defined as one of the central programming units used in the development of Python.

Another similarity the first release bore with Module-3 is found in the exception model which comes with an added else clause. With the public release of this early version came a flurry of users which culminated in the formation of a primary discussion forum for Python in 1994. The group was named comp.lang.python and served as a milestone for the growing popularity of Python users.

Following the release of the first version in the 29th of February, 1991, there were seven other updates made to the early version 0.9.0. These updates took varying tags under the 0.9.0 version and were spread out over nearly three years (1991 to 1993). The first version update came in the form of Python 0.9.1, which was released in the same month of February 1991 as its predecessor. The next update came in the autumn period of the release year, under the label Python 0.9.2. By Christmas Eve of the same year (1991) python published its third update to the earliest version under the label Python 0.9.4. By January of the succeeding year, the 2nd precisely, a gift update under the label Python 0.9.5 was released. By the 6th of April, 1992, a sixth update followed named, Python 0.9.6. It wasn't until the next year, 1993, that a seventh update was released under the tag Python 0.9.8. The eighth and final update to the earliest version came five months after the seventh, on the 29th of July, 1993, and was dubbed python 0.9.9.

These updates marked the first generation of python development before it transcended into the next version label.

- **Python 1.0**

After the last update to Python 0.9.0, a new version, Python 1.0, was released in January of the following year. 1994 marked the addition of key new features to the Python programming language. Functional programming tools such as map, reduce, filter, and lambda were part of the new features of the version 1 release. Van Rossum mentioned that the obtainment of map, lambda, reduce and filter was made possible by a LISP hacker who missed them and submitted patches that worked. Van Rossum's contract with CWI came to an end with the release of the first update version 1.2 on the 10th of April, 1995. In the same year, Van Rossum went on to join CNRI (Corporation for National Research Initiatives) in Reston, Virginia, United States, where he continued to work on Python and published different version updates.

Nearly six months following the first version update, version 1.3 was released on the 12th of October, 1995. The third update, version 1.4, came almost a year later in October of 1996. By then, Python had developed numerous added features. Some of the typical new features included an inbuilt support system for complex numbers and keyword arguments which, although inspired by Modula-3, shared a bit of a likeness to the keyword arguments of Common Lisp. Another included feature was a simple form hiding data through name mangling, although it could be easily bypassed.

It was during his days at CNRI that Van Rossum began the CP4E (Computer Programming for Everybody) program which was aimed at making more people get easy access to programming by engaging in simple literacy of programming languages. Python was a pivotal element to van Rossum's campaign, and owing to its concentration on clean forms of syntax; Python was an already suitable programming language. Also, since the goals of ABC and CP4E were quite similar, there was no hassle putting Python to use. The program was pitched to and funded by DARPA, although it did become inactive in 2007 after running for eight years. However, Python still tries to be relatively easy to learn by not being too arcane in its semantics and syntax, although no priority is made of reaching out to non-programmers again.

The year 2000 marked another significant step in the development of Python when the python core development team switched to a new platform — BeOpen.com where a new group, BeOpen PythonLabs team was formed. At the request of CNRI, a new version update 1.6 was released on the 5th of September, succeeding the fourth version update (Python 1.5) on the December of 1997. This update marked the complete cycle of development for the programming language at CNRI because the development team left shortly afterward. This change affected the timelines of release for the new version Python 2.0 and the version 1.6 update; causing them to clash. It was only a question of time before Van Rossum, and his crew of PythonLabs developers switched to Digital Creations, with Python 2.0 as the only version ever released by BeOpen.com.

With the version 1.6 release caught between a switch of platforms, it didn't take long for CNRI to include a license in the version release of Python 1.6. The license contained in the release was quite more prolonged than the previously used CWI license, and it featured a clause mentioning that the license was under the protection of the laws applicable to the State of Virginia. This intervention sparked a legal feud which led The Free Software Foundation into a debate regarding the "choice-of-law" clause being incongruous with that if the GNU General Public License. At this point, there was a call to negotiations between FSF, CNRI, and BeOoen regarding changing to Python's free software license which would serve to make it compatible with GPL. The negotiation process resulted in the release of another version update under the name of Python 1.6.1. This new version was no different from its predecessor in any way asides a few new bug fixes and the newly added GPL-compatible license.

- **Python 2.0:**

After the many legal dramas surrounding the release of the second-generation Python 1.0 which corroborated into the release of an unplanned update (version 1.6.1), Python was keen to put all behind and forge ahead. So, in October of 2000, Python 2.0 was released. The new release featured new additions such as list comprehensions which were obtained from other functional programming languages Haskell and SETL. The syntax of this latest version was akin to that found in Haskell, but different in that Haskell used punctuation characters while Python stuck to alphabetic keywords.

Python 2.0 also featured a garbage collection system which was able to collect close reference cycles. A version update (Python 2.1) quickly followed the release of Python 2.0, as did Python

1.6.1. However, due to the legal issue over licensing, Python renamed the license on the new release to Python Software Foundation License. As such, every new specification, code or documentation added from the release of version update 2.1 was owned and protected by the PSF (Python Software Foundation) which was a nonprofit organization created in the year 2001. The organization was designed similarly to the Apache Software Foundation. The release of version 2.1 came with changes made to the language specifications, allowing support of nested scopes such as other statically scoped languages. However, this feature was, by default, not in use and unrequired until the release of the next update, version 2.2 on the 21st of December, 2001.

Python 2.2 came with a significant innovation of its own in the form of a unification of all Python's types and classes. The unification process merged the types coded in C and the classes coded in Python into a single hierarchy. The unification process caused Python's object model to remain totally and continuously object-oriented. Another significant innovation was the addition of generators as inspired by Icon. Two years after the release of version 2.2, version 2.3 was published in July of 2003. It was nearly another two years before version 2.4 was released on the 30th of November in 2004. Version 2.5 came less than a year after Python 2.4, in September of 2006. This version introduced a "with" statement containing a code block in a context manager; as in obtaining a lock before running the code block and releasing the lock after that or opening and closing a file. The block of code made for behavior similar to RAII (Resource Acquisition Is Initialization) and swapped the typical "try" or "finally" idiom.

The release of version 2.6 on the 1st of October, 2008 was strategically scheduled such that it coincided with the release of

Python 3.0. Asides the proximity in release date, version 2.6 also had some new features like the "warnings" mode which outlined the use of elements which had been omitted from Python 3.0. Subsequently, in July of 2010, another update to Python 2.0 was released in the version of python 2.7. The new version updates shared features and coincided in release with version 3.1 — the first version update of python 3. At this time, Python drew an end to the release of Parallel 2.x and 3.x, making python 2.7 the last version update of the 2.x series. Python went public in 2014, November precisely, to announce to its username that the availability of python 2.7 would stretch until 2020. However, users were advised to switch to python 3 in their earliest convenience.

- **Python 3.0:**

The fourth generation of Python, Python 3.0, otherwise known as Py3K and python 3000, was published on the 3rd of December 2008. This version was designed to fix the fundamental flaws in the design system of the scripting language. A new version number had to be made to implement the required changes which could not be run while keeping the stock compatibility of the 2.x series that was by this time redundant. The guiding rule for the creation of python 3 was to limit the duplication of features by taking out old formats of processing stuff. Otherwise, Python three still followed the philosophy with which the previous versions were made. Albeit, as Python had evolved to accumulate new but redundant ways of programming alike tasks, python 3.0 was emphatically targeted at quelling duplicative modules and constructs in keeping with the philosophy of making one "and

preferably only one" apparent way of doing things. Regardless of these changes, though, version 3.0 maintained a multi-paradigm language, even though it didn't share compatibility with its predecessor.

The lack of compatibility meant Python 2.0 codes were unable to be run on python 3.0 without proper modifications. The dynamic typing used in Python as well as the intention to change the semantics of specific methods of dictionaries, for instance, made a perfect mechanical conversion from the 2.x series to version 3.0 very challenging. A tool, name of 2to3, was created to handle the parts of translation which could be automatically done. It carried out its tasks quite successfully, even though an early review stated that the tool was incapable of handling certain aspects of the conversion process. Proceeding the release of version 3.0, projects that required compatible with both the 2.x and 3.x series were advised to be given a singular base for the 2.x series. The 3.x series platform, on the other hand, was to produce releases via the 2to3 tool.

For a long time, editing the Python 3.0 codes were forbidden because they required being run on the 2.x series. However, now, it is no longer necessary. The reason being that in 2012, the recommended method was to create a single code base which could run under the 2.x and 3.x series through compatibility modules. Between the December of 2008 and July 2019, 8 version updates have been published under the python 3.x series. The current version as at the 8th of July 2019 is the Python 3.7.4. Within this timeframe, many updates have been made to the programming language, involving the addition of new features mentioned below:

1. Print which used to be a statement was changed to an inbuilt function, making it relatively easier to swap out a module in utilizing different print functions as well as regularizing the syntax. In the late versions of the 2.x series, (python 2.6 and 2.7), print is introduced as inbuilt, but is concealed by a syntax of the print statement which is capable of being disabled by entering the following line of code into the top of the file: from__future__import print_function
2. The [input] function in the Python 2.x series was removed, and the [raw_input] function to [input] was renamed. The change was such that the [input] function of Python 3 behaves similarly to the [raw_input] function of the python 2.x series; meaning input is typically outputted in the form of strings instead of being evaluated as a single expression.
3. [reduce] was removed with the exemption of [map] and [filter] from the in-built namespace into [functools]. The reason behind this change is that

operations involving [reduce] are better expressed with the use of an accumulation loop.

4. Added support was provided for optional function annotations which could be used in informal type declarations as well as other purposes.
5. The [str]/[unicode] types were unified, texts represented, and immutable bytes type were introduced separately as well as a mutable [bytearray] type which was mostly corresponding; both of which indicate several arrays of bytes.
6. Taking out the backward-compatibility features such as implicit relative imports, old-style classes, and string exceptions.
7. Changing the mode of integer division functionality. For instance, in the Python 2.x series, 5/2 equals 2. Note that in the 3.x series, 5/2 equals 2.5. From the recent versions of the 2.x series beginning from version 2.2 up until python 3: 5//2 equals 2.

In contemporary times, version releases in the version 3.x series have all been equipped with added, substantial new features; and every ongoing development on Python is being done in line with the 3.x series.

C. HOW TO DOWNLOAD AND INSTALL PYTHON

In this time and age, being techy is a demand of the times, and the lack of knowledge, classifies one as an outback. This can result to being left out from the career world, especially in the field of programming.

Numerous big shot companies have employed their own programmers for purposes of branding, and to cut back on IT expenses.

In the world of programming, using Python language is found to be easier and programmer-friendly, thus, the universal use.

Discussed below are information on how to download python for MS Windows. In this particular demo, we have chosen windows because it's the most common worldwide – even in not so progressive countries. We want to cater to the programming needs of everyone all over the globe.

Python 2.7.12 version was selected because this version bridges the gap between the old version 2 and the new version 3.

Some of the updated functions/applications of version 3 are still not compatible with some devices, so 2.7.12 is a smart choice.

Steps in downloading Python 2.7.12, and installing it on Windows

1. Type python on your browser and press the Search button to display the search results.

Scroll down to find the item you are interested in. In this instance, you are looking for python. click “python releases for windows”, and a new page opens. See image below:

2. Select the Python version, python 2.7.12, and click, or you can select the version that is compatible to your device or OS.

Python Releases for Windows

- Latest Python 2 Release - Python 2.7.12
- Latest Python 3 Release - Python 3.5.2

- Python 3.6.0b1 - 2016-09-12
  - Download Windows x86 web-based installer
  - Download Windows x86 executable installer
  - Download Windows x86 embeddable zip file
  - Download Windows x86-64 web-based installer
  - Download Windows x86-64 executable installer
  - Download Windows x86-64 embeddable zip file
  - Download Windows help file
- Python 3.6.0a4 - 2016-08-15
  - Download Windows x86 web-based installer
  - Download Windows x86 executable installer
  - Download Windows x86 embeddable zip file
  - Download Windows x86-64 web-based installer
  - Download Windows x86-64 executable installer
  - Download Windows x86-64 embeddable zip file

3. The new page contains the various python types. Scroll down and select an option: in this instance, select Windows x86 MSI installer and click.

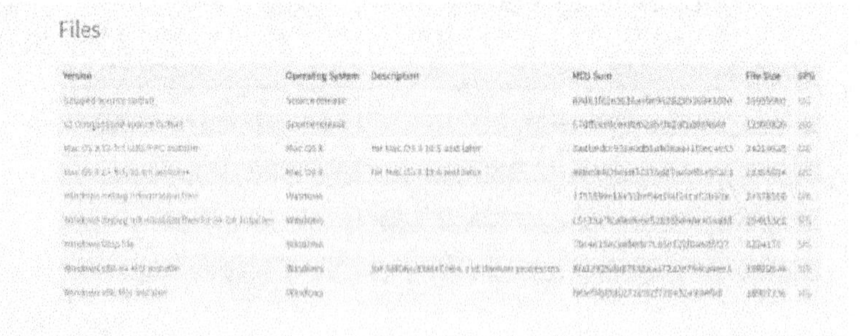

4. Press the Python box at the bottom of your screen.

Click the "Run" button, and wait for the new window to appear.

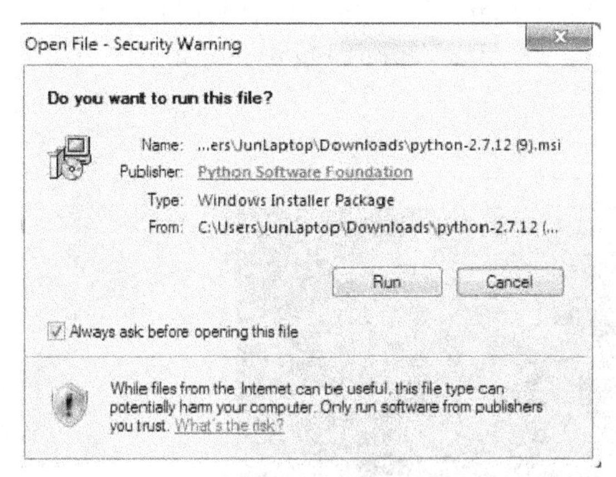

5. Select the user options that you require and press "NEXT".

Your screen will display the hard drive where your python will be located.

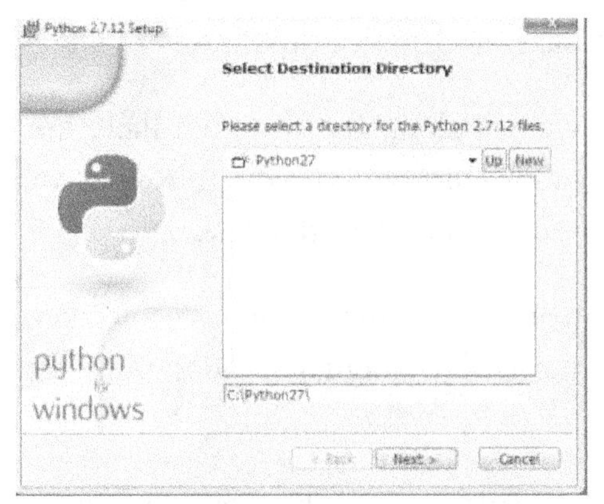

6. Press the "NEXT" button.

7. Press yes, and wait for a few minutes. Sometimes it can take longer for the application to download, depending on the speed of your internet.
8. After that, click the FINISHED button to signify that the installation has been completed

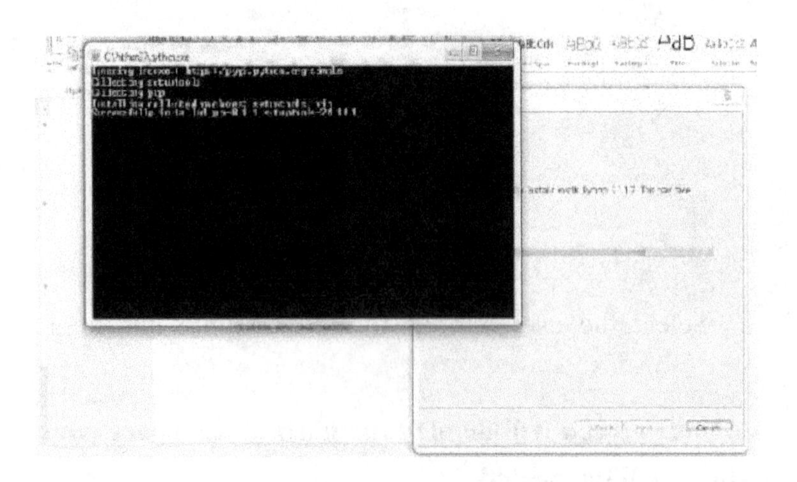

Your python has been installed in your computer and is now ready to use. Find it in drive C, or wherever you have saved it.

There can be glitches along the way, but there are options which are presented in this article. If you follow it well, there is no reason that you cannot perform this task.

It's important to note that there's no need to compile programs. Python is an interpretive language and can execute quickly your commands.

You can also download directly from the Python website, by selecting any of these versions – 3.5.2 or 2.7.12. and clicking ‘download’. (For this book, 2.7.12 is used, in general, for easy discussions).

See image below:

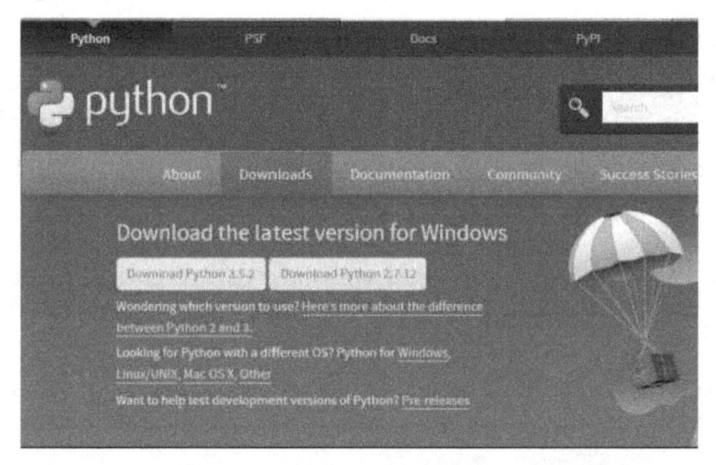

Follow the step by step instructions prompted by the program itself. Save and run the program in your computer.

For Mac

To download Python on Mac, you can follow a similar procedure, but this time, you will have to access the “Python.mpkg” file, to run the installer.

For Linux

For Linux, Python 2 and 3 may have been installed by default. Hence, check first your operating system. You can check if your device has already a Python program, by accessing your command prompt and entering this: python—version, or python3—version.

If Python is not installed in your Linux, the result "command not found" will be displayed. You may want to download both Python 2.7.12 and any of the versions of Python 3 for your Linux. This is due to the fact that Linux can have more compatibility with Python 3.

For windows users, now that you have downloaded the program, you're ready to start.

And yes, congratulations! You can now begin working and having fun with your Python programming system.

D. WRITING THE FIRST PYTHON PROGRAM

Beginners may find it difficult to start using Python. It's a given and nothing's wrong about that. However, your desire to learn will make it easier for you to gradually become familiar with the language.

Here are the specific steps you can follow to start using Python.

Steps in using Python

Step #1–Read all about Python.

Python has included a README information in your downloaded version. It's advisable to read it first, so you will learn more about the program.

You can start using your Python through the command box (black box), or you can go to your saved file and read first the README file by clicking it.

See image below:

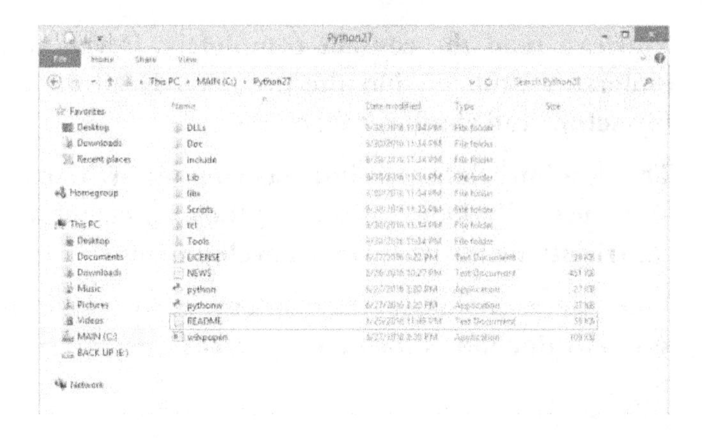

This box will appear.

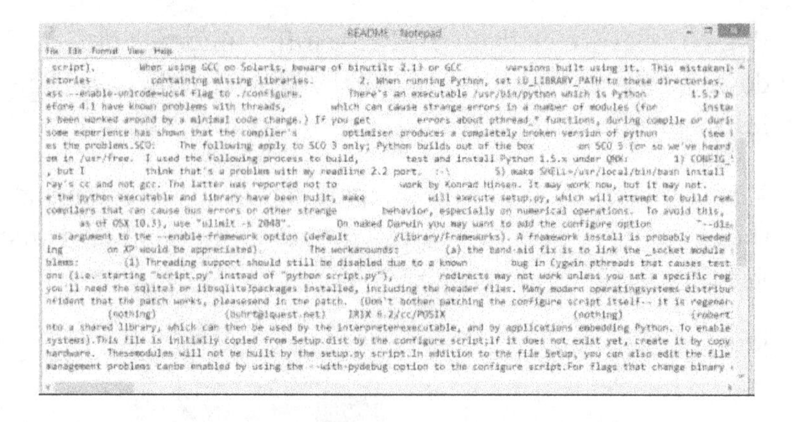

You can read the content completely, if you want to understand more what the program is all about, the file-setup, and similar information.

This is a long data that informs you of how to navigate and use Python. Also, Python welcomes new contributions for its further development.

You can copy paste the content of the box into a Window document for better presentation.

If you don't want to know all the other information about Python and you're raring to go, you can follow these next steps.

Step #2–Start using Python.

First open the Python file you have saved in your computer. Click on Python as show below. In some versions, you just click 'python'for the shell to appear.

See image below:

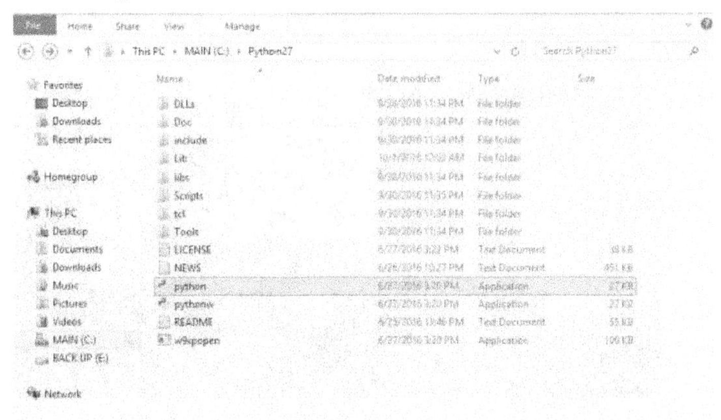

You can start using Python by utilizingthe simplest function, which is'print'.It's the simplest statement or directive of python. It prints a line or string that you specify.

For Python 2, print command may or may not be enclosed in parenthesis or brackets, while in Python 3 you have to enclose print with brackets.

Example for Python 2:

print "Welcome to My Corner."

Example for Python 3:

print ("Welcome to My Corner")

The image below shows what appears when you press'enter'.

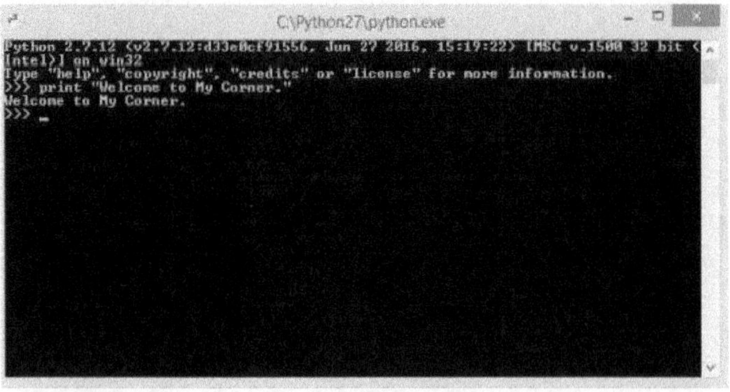

You may opt to use a Python shell through idle. If you do, this is how it would appear:

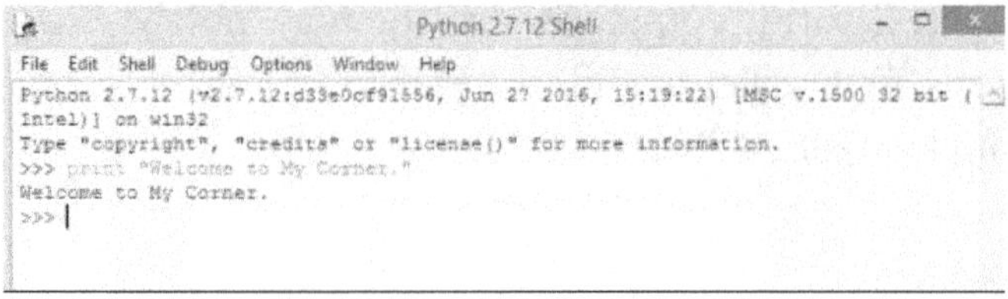

In the Python 3.5.2 version, the text colors are: function (purple), string (green) and the result (blue). (The string is composed of the words inside the bracket ("Welcome to My Corner"), while the function is the command word outside the bracket (print).

Take note that the image above is from the Python 2.7.12 version.

You have to use indentation for your Python statements/codes. The standard Python code uses four spaces. The indentations are used in place of braces or blocks.

In some programming languages, you usually use semi-colons at the end of the commands–in python, you don't need to add semi-colons at the end of the whole statement.

In Python, semi-colons are used in separating variables inside the brackets.

For version 3, click on your downloaded Python program and save the file in your computer. Then Click on IDLE (Integrated DeveLopment Environment), your shell will appear. You can now start using your Python.It's preferable to use idle, so that your codes can be interpreted directly by idle.

Alternative method to open a shell (for some versions).

An alternative method to use your Python is to open a shell through the following steps:

Step #1– Open your menu.

After downloading and saving your Python program in your computer, open your menu and find your saved Python file. You may find it in the downloaded files of your computer or in the files where you saved it.

Step #2–Access your Python file.

Open your saved Python file (Python 27) by double clicking it. The contents of Python 27 will appear. Instead of clicking on Python directly (as shown above), click on Lib instead. See image below.

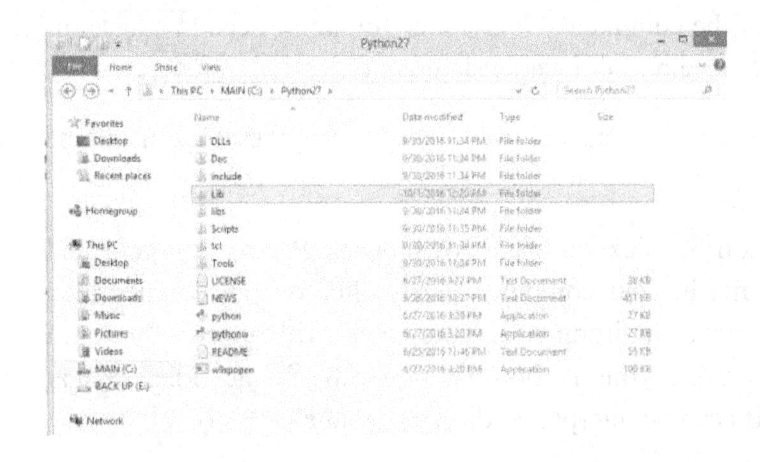

This will appear:

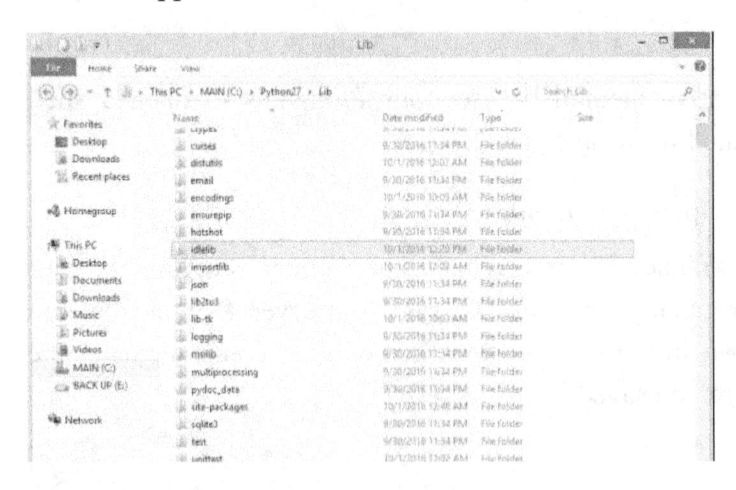

Step #3–Click on'idlelib'.

Clicking the'idlelib'will show this content:

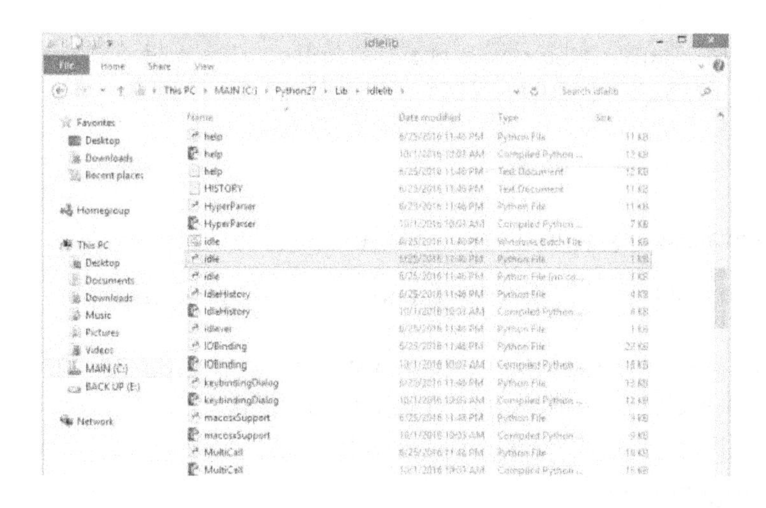

Step #4–Click on idle to show the Python shell.

When you click on any of the 'idle' displayed on the menu, the'white'shell will be displayed, as shown below:

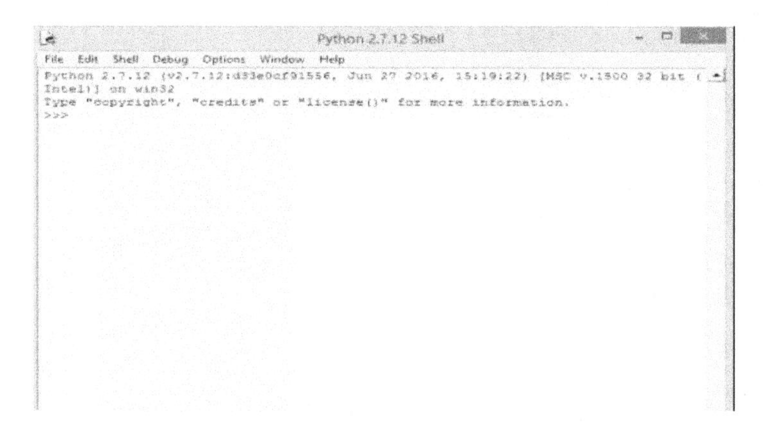

The differences between the three'idle'menu, is that the first two'idle'commands have the black box (shell) too, while the last‘idle’has only the‘white’box (shell). I prefer the third‘idle’because it’s easy to use.

Step #5–Start using your Python shell.

You can now start typing Python functions, using the shell above.

You may have noticed that there are various entries to the contents of each of the files that you have opened. You can click and open all of them, as you progress in learning more about your Python programming.

Python is a programming language that has been studied by students for several days or months. Thus, what’s presented in this book are the basics for beginners.

CHAPTER 2. BASIC OF PYTHON

Python can be used as an active translator or transcriber by interaction through the web. It can also be employed to formulate lessons. In interaction, though, there is one serious concern: that is, it is impossible to keep a copy of what transpired. On the other hand, using lessons allows you to keep a record of the work done. In the interactive translator, you are allowed to open only one display page, while in lessons, you can open as many as you need.

Variables

Python uses information that are not constant, these are used to keep the data. When using these, be sure to put descriptions. These data could be names, age, addresses, gender and other similar material.

Outputs and Inputs

Any computer program requires interfacing between itself and the person using it. The user encodes and that is input, and the output is printing what has been encoded.

Mathematics

Numbers are the common language in computer programs including Python. Mathematical operations are used by Python as you will learn later on. Most of its language are represented by mathematical equations and symbols.

Loop

You need to understand the term loop in python. It is a symbol used to represent repeated word/s or sentence/s in python programming. Anything that is being repeatedly used can employ a loop.

Python categories

It is important to be acquainted with the types of python product categories for easy reference and understanding. Python categories are symbolized by A, B, C that signifies the shifts in language. Examples are 3.3.1 to 3.3.2. This means there are minor changes, but when it employs something like 2.xx to 3.xx it means there are major changes.

Cutting

This is a critical component of python which is used to copy the desired part of a data. It is a method of making programs simple by concentrating on items from a gamut of data. When you do that, you are actually removing components that are not relevant to the program.

Modules

Modules are files of descriptions and declarations of Python. It is a list of all the terminologies used by python with corresponding explanations of each. Python adopts a method of consolidating definitions into one folder called **module**. These modules can be introduced into different modules depending on the needs of the programmer or user.

This is created to allow users to have a better understanding and easy access to the standard library of Python. A programmer or even a beginner can make modules for his use.

Modules can be on: Indexing and searching, Audio and Music, Web development, Console and Database. Python provides an array of modules that you can use. You can also make your own.

Source codes

Generating Python source codes can be tedious,if you don't know how to derive your codes.

Program developers have now an application that converts your Python 2 codes to Python version 3 codes from AST.

You can create your own code as discussed in the chapters, and it's easy to append strings to a list to create a code, but it won't hurt you, if you know how to generate Python source codes. One way of doing this is to use context managers.

These are the most basic elements in python, there are more but with the ones presented, one can already start using python and learn the others, as you go on in your programming.

CHAPTER 3. FULL INSTRUCTIONS ON HOW TO CODE

We have touched on this first topic already, but we will expand and reiterate here. First up is naming conventions.

Comments

Here are some best practices for your comments that will help other readers understand you easier:

- Start with a summary of the sketch and what it will accomplish. Provide any links if it helps the understanding of your design. Try to approach your block comments from a user-friendly stance as much as possible to give a clear idea of what you will be doing.
- Write in the active voice. Use a clear, conversational tone for your writing, as if you were speaking to another person standing next to you.
- For instructions to the user, use the second person, to invoke in the user that they should be the ones to carry out your instructions.
- Use short descriptive phrases rather than complex phrases. It is easier to understand one simple idea at a time.
- Be explicit about what you are doing with your actions. For example: "Next, you'll read the value of the sensor on pin **thisPin**."
- Avoid phrases or words that are 'fluff' or do not contribute to the explanation, e.g. you see, you'd want

to, etc. Instead, skip those words and give a statement that's direct to the point, e.g. set the pins.

- Check your assumptions, make sure you have explained all of your ideas and haven't left something that can only be explained 'in your head.'
- Give a description for every variable or constant with a comment of its purpose either before, or in line with the variable or constant.
- Similarly, give an explanation of a block of code that you're about to perform before the instructions are executed, so it's clear what's about to happen.
- Every loop should have comments explaining why this loop exists (e.g. what it is doing), and a verbal explanation of its condition if it's still not clear.

Coding Best Practices

- **Follow naming conventions**

Do not create one letter variable names! Your naming conventions exist so that you can, at a glance, read your code without having to refer to other places to understand what is going on.

- **Write code that is reusable or modular**

User-defined functions are a great way to accomplish this. By doing this, you can write a segment of code in just one place and refer to it each time it is necessary. This makes better sense and is much cleaner and simpler to read.

- **Write a flow-chart of your sketch** before you start coding

Seriously, this cannot be overstated how valuable this step is to write clean code. By knowing all the pieces you will need to accomplish your sketch's task ahead of time conceptually, you can successfully plan ahead and use things like functions in a smart way.

- **Keep things organize and together**

If you make a function to smooth an analog sensor, make sure that's all it does. Don't start doing other parts of your code within that function. If your function needs to, you can have it call yet another function to help it accomplish its task. Again think modular (small pieces make a big part).

- **Make yourself a toolbox**

Make functions that do specific things. Then use your tools as needed in your code.

- **Keep your sketches**

Even if you think you won't need a sketch you made anymore, keep them. If you need a piece of code that you've already written for another project and you have followed these practices, you can simply snag that piece of code and drop it into the new project you're working on. Brilliant!

- **Write your functions in a generalized way whenever possible for these exact reasons**

To put this simply, it means that if you were making a function to draw a square, make a function to draw a rectangle instead since a square is a special case of a rectangle, where the edges are equal.

- **Make sure your functions do what they** say **they will do**

E.g., if it is a function named 'flickerLeds' (**pinValue**), it better be flickering some LEDs!

- **Avoid pointers**

We didn't even touch on them in this document, and we are only going to tell you they exist to tell you not to use them unless you're an advanced user. They are the most likely 'tool' to cause the crazy, bad kinds of problems from happening in your coding, and are notoriously tough for a beginner to use properly. So avoid them until you are sure you know what you are doing.

- **Embrace self-improvement**

Understand from day 1 that as a fledgling coder that you will grow and improve over time. Use each challenge you come across to try writing new sketches as an opportunity to grow and hone your skills.

- **Reach out to the community for help and advice!**

There are some really fantastic people in our big community of hobbyists that are willing to help you learn and grow as an enthusiast. This is a great way to meet friends and learn so many new ways to do things you may not have thought about previously.

- **Try to make things foolproof when you code**

Try to make sure your for loops terminate, try to account for unexpected inputs when checking values, try to constrain your data within expected values. These 'tedious' steps are what keeps your program running smooth and bug-free!

- **Know how to use debugging tools and techniques**

It's a more advanced topic but learning about debugging tools and techniques for large-scale projects such as robotics, or as a controller for something like a pump mechanism will help expand your knowledge further.

- **Write both brackets or both braces at the start then fill in the date in-between**

When writing functions, loops or anything with brackets and braces, this trick helps to ensure that you will be closing all of your brackets and braces, preventing unexpected results.

- **Try new ways to use your Arduino!**

This is how you can really develop new skills. When you have more skills, you can think of even more things you can do with the chip! The possibilities with this micro-controller are nearly limitless and are bound only by the limits of your imagination.

More Naming Best Practices

- **Functions follow the same rules as variables**

The name should start with a lower-case letter, all one word, and additional words are distinguished with capital letters.

- **Functions should use verb names to describe their function**

E.g. **stepMotor(), getValue(), smoothReadings()**, etc. All these names explain with an action word what this function should be doing.

- **Make the name describe the purpose of the function**

- **Make sure the for loop variables are clear on what they represent**

Having a variable of **x** can work, but it really offers nothing to the person reading your code for them to understand exactly what that variable is for.

CHAPTER 4. HOW TO MAKE PREDICTIONS WITH ALGORITHM

How are you feeling at this stage? Have you encountered any errors? Are you feeling as if you have gained some new knowledge?

Hopefully, things are going smoothly and you are grasping the concepts well at this point. Let's take a look at how to make predictions with algorithms in Python and what it means.

WHAT IS PREDICTIVE ANALYSTICS?

"Predictive Analysis" is regularly talked about with regards to building information, for instance, originating from instruments, specific sensors and associated frameworks in the real world. Business data, at an organization, for example, may incorporate exchange information, deals results, client dissensions, and promote data. Progressively, organizations settle on information-driven choices in light of this important aggregation of data.

With a significant growth in competition, organizations look for a competitive advantage in bringing items and administrations to open markets. Information-focused models typically enable organizations to take care of long-standing issues in creative and unique ways.

Manufacturers, for instance, often think that it is difficult to enhance just its equipment. Item designers can add prescient abilities to existing answers for increased incentives to the client. Utilizing prescient examination for hardware upkeep, or prescient support, can predict future product development disappointments, figure vitality accurately, and decrease working expenses. For instance, sensors that measure certain wave patterns and vibrations in car parts, and in turn, flag the requirements for upkeep before the car/automobile flops during use by an actual consumer.

Additionally, organizations utilize a prescient investigation to make more exact predictions, for example, estimating the increased demand for power on the electrical grids. These figures enable companies to do asset planning, like looking for other power plants, in order to be more efficient and effective.

To extricate an increase in value from all of the information, organizations apply calculations to vast information sets, utilizing new and upcoming technology tools, for example, Hadoop. The information sources may comprise value-based databases, hardware log files, pictures, audio/video, sensory details, or a number of other kinds of information. True innovation is often the result of using and combining data from a variety of different sources.

With this information, these technologies are of critical importance in the discovery of trends and patterns. Machine learning methods are utilized to discover commonalities and patterns in information and to estimate what the outcomes are going to be.

What does Predictive analysis do? What does it mean?

Predictable analytics allows groups in different job roles, ranging from financial, healthcare workers in pharmacy industries, and automobile. This particular analytical process is how we utilize the data that we have analyzed in order to make viable guesses which are largely based on the analyzed information.

Whew! Don't panic.

The great thing is that this process is a predictive model which allows for a systematic approach of delivering outcomes based on a certain set of common criteria.

To define what "predictive analytics" means, this process involves applying a certain statistical approach based on Python machine learning strategies and models which creates realistic and measurable estimations and predictions about future outcomes. Regularly, Python machine learning techniques are used in real-world problem-solving. For example, it is commonly used to estimate the value of something in the near future such as "**How long can my word processor run before needing it to be replaced or require routine maintenance?**"

Constructed on a set of criteria, it can also be used to guess certain customer behaviors. A great deal of banks and financial institutions use this to determine the creditworthiness of their customers, how likely they are to default on their mortgage or car loan, or the probability of excessive overdrafts each month. It's pretty amazing.

Predictive analytics is primarily used in helping companies and organizations make future predictions and meet certain goals. Think about the most common goals of any business: stay in business, make money, and reduce excess waste through the analyzing of data, methods decrease expenses and ability to offer employee bonuses if goals are met. To do something of this scale does require an extensive amount of various data types and inputting them into pre-built models that will ultimately generate concise, measurable, and most importantly—achievable outcomes to maintain a positive bottom line and support growth.

In order to make this click, let's look back at what we said: "predictive analysis" is and what it's for, as it relates to some real-world examples. These are not all inclusive by any means, and more can be found using a simple Google search and research.

Real World Examples of Predictive Analytics:

The Car Industry–Breakthrough technology in cars, designed to gather specific details and information regarding how fast the car is going, how far the car has traveled, its emission levels and the behaviors of drivers are now used with an extremely sophisticated predictive analysis model. This allows the analysts to release extremely beneficial data for car manufacturers, insurance companies, and the racing circles.

Aviation–Determining the viability and health of an aircraft is an application developed by an aviation engineer, it helped improve the performance of aircraft speed and reduce costs to maintain and repair them. This particular application is used to test performance in every critical function of the plan from the take-off, to the control systems, all the way to the efficiency of the fuel and maximum take-off conditions.

The Production of Energy–Electricity companies use predictive analytics in order to determine the cost and demand for electrical supplies. There are a ton of extremely sophisticated models that forecast access, patterns (future and past), the different changes in weather and many other factors.

Accounting and Financial Services–The Development of credit risk models is a prime example of predictive analytics in the real world. Nowadays, banks, credit unions, and many other financial institutions use these models and applications in order to determine a customer or potential client's credit risk.

Equipment and Machine Manufacturing—Testing and determining future machine weaknesses and failures. This particular application is used in helping to improve the efficiency of assembly lines and production of large equipment and machines and at the same time optimizing its operations and workforce.

Modern Medicine–This is last on the list, but certainly not least. Predictive analysis has been used in modern medicine to detect infections and common diseases and even pre-existing conditions. It's also a great way to bridge the communication gaps between those in the medical profession.

Pretty cool, huh? Can you find more ways that predictive analysis is used in real-world situations to improve our life, our economy, and our businesses?

WORKFLOW IN PREDICTIVE ANALYSTICS:

You may or may not be familiar with predictive models at this stage of your learning, but you can think of a real-world example as to what meteorologists use in day to day weather forecasting.

A basic industry utilization of prescient models identifies with any circuit that consumes power and allows a prediction to be made about the demand for power, as it relates here—energy. For this model, network administrators and brokers require precise conjectures of each circuit load to make important choices for integrating them into the electrical grid framework. Huge amounts of information are easily accessible and utilizing these prescient analytics, allowing matrix administrators to transform this data into noteworthy bits of knowledge that can be used to make important decisions and predictions.

Typically, a simple workflow for a predictive analytics model will follow these basic steps outlined here:

- Import information from changed sources, for example, web chronicles, databases, and spreadsheets.
- Information sources incorporate energy load data and information in a CSV record and national climate information demonstrating temperatures and varying dew points.
- Clean the information by evacuating anomalies and joining information sources.
- Distinguish information spikes; especially pinpoint missing information, or even bizarre outputs to expel from the information.
- Make a solitary table including energy load, temperature and dew point.
- Build a precise data model in light of the accumulated information.
- Predicting any type of energy source is a perplexing procedure with numerous factors. You may utilize neural systems to assemble and prepare a prescient model.
- Practice training through your data index to achieve diverse strategies. At the point when the preparation

is finished, you can attempt the model against new information to perceive how well it performs.

- Coordinate the model into a front gauging framework in a production type of environment.
- When you locate a model that precisely gauges the outcomes, you can move it into your creation framework, making the examination accessible to programming projects or gadgets, including web applications, servers, or smartphones.

Your aggregated data tells a tale that is certainly complex. To withdraw the insights, you are going to need an extremely accurate design which is predictive. This might not be the best step as a beginner; nonetheless, it is here for reference to the entire picture of Python capabilities.

Predictive analysis is being modeled after major mathematical models to predict a conference or result. These designs forecast the desired outcome at some future time based on modifications placed into data inputs. Using a repetitive procedure, you create the models by choosing a training information set where you will proceed to test and further validate the information. After you examine it to ascertain its reliability and accuracy in predicting forecasts, play around with different methods until you find one that is comfortable for you. The important thing is that you choose one that you can understand, learn and apply without much effort.

To give you an idea of some good examples of such a method, you can try a time-series reversal model for predicting low and even high levels of flight traffic or fuel. Of course, this is certainly predicting based on a linear approach to speed compared to upload and continuing to be extremely beneficial in real-world estimation models for conjecture.

WHAT IS DIFFERENCE BETWEEN PREDICTIVE ANALYSTICS & PRESCRIPTIVE ANALYSTICS?

Businesses that have been able to successfully implement predictive analytics have a competitive advantage to problems, situations and good things in the future. Predictive analytics is a process that creates an estimation of what will happen next—literally. It also gives you tips simple about how to be able to make high-level decisions in a way that maximizes the information you wouldn't have access to.

Prescriptive analytics is just a branch of data analytics that makes use of designs that are predictive guesses to make for the most ideal outcomes. Prescriptive examination depends on advancement and tenets-based procedures for decision-making on a most basic of levels. Anticipating any issues or strains on the framework is absolutely essential in the decision-making process. It means what is to be done is based on the prediction.

CHAPTER 5. INTRODUCTION TO BASIC DATA TYPES

In this Chapter, we will discuss data types, Python implementations, and standard data. I am sure that after reading this Chapter and the book, you will be able to create a program that will allow users to use Python methods and logic to manipulate numbers. All programming languages execute a program differently, and this is the reason for learning different ways of organizing words and separate statements according to the program to avoid experiencing some errors in your code. This chapter will discuss how Python execute commands and how the whole program operates. Working with Python is like dealing with interpreted programming language because of the text interpreter, which enables you to read the content faster. Text interpreter also helps you to quickly understand how to code correctly for the program to run effectively.

In addition to interpreting words, Python is a scripting language that allows programmers to write out the scripts and use extension .py to save them, or even write them and execute all the statements into different Python shell. In fact, Python will compile your program into a byte code just like Java byte code. An excellent example of what Python can compile is the source code, thus makes it easy for Python to execute the code in a short time.

Additionally, you can save byte code files into __pycache__, a subdirectory found in the directory which keeps the file sources. If you write out john.py, for example, it will rename it as john.pyc once it is converted into the byte codes. A programmer can manually compile the code if he/she experiences some problem in running the program. Since Python will carry out this process by itself it is not an issue to the beginners. Usually, Python confirms if there is a compiled version of the .pyc suffix or not when loading in the byte code. Ensure that the file is newer to enable the program to run effectively. Also, Python will create your byte code if it does not exist to execute the program.

IMPLEMENTATION OF PYTHON

Although this might be seen as a new thing, implementation of Python refers to the environment and the program that facilitates the execution of your program within the Python language, and it is represented with CPython. Depending on the type of the CPython you are using, such environment enables you to execute different kinds of the codes and statements you are handling within the program.

In programming, implementation includes everything to enable you to work on your program and complete it successfully on time. Unlike in other programming languages, implementation helps the programmers to get more things done in Python. The Python enables you to work on your program with many different programming languages like Java and C++, and this makes it appealing and straightforward.

Apart from CPython, you can use implementations such as Brython, CLPython, HotPy, IronPython, Jython, PyMite, and PyPy in Python to carry out the specific thing with the Python language. For the beginners, Python is the most suitable for them because it is not confusing like the other programming languages.

STANDARD DATA

Python programming language is suitable for those who are looking for the programming language that will enable them to work on their project using many different data successfully. These data are used to define various operations which the programmers can use to do multiple things when coding. There are five types of data in Python, and these include Numbers, Dictionary, Tuple, List, and String. These data types are essential in programming. You can use any of them to increase the function and the speed of the Python.

Additionally, number data types stores the numerical values and are created as objects after assigning a value to them. Numerical values exist in four types, namely; assigned integers, complex numbers, float point, and long integers shown as octal or hexadecimal. As a programmer, you should use these types of numerical values correctly to ensure that there is no error when running the program. Although Python allows a programmer to use the lowercase mainly when dealing with the long type of number, it is good to use uppercase when working with the letter as it eliminates any confusion the programmer can experience in reading the program.

Because Python is a programming tool that helps individuals to use and read it with ease, it is the best method one should start with when he/she enters programming professional. It is easy to use and read as it has syntax, which allows programmers to express their concepts without necessarily creating a coding page. Generally, Python is the best language for you due to its usability and readability. We are sure that after reading this book, you can now create a program with Python programming language.

CHAPTER 6. INTERMEDIATE AND ADVANCED DATA TYPES

In Python, every value is assigned a specified datatype. Since every aspect of Python consists of an object, data types are in fact classes, and variables are instances or objects of these classes. Python has several data types used in its operations. Listed below are some of the basic, important ones.

PYTHON NUMBERS:

Python numbers is a category constituted by floating-point numbers and integers as well as complex numbers. They are usually defined as int (integer), float (floating number), and complex (complex numbers) class in Python. To determine the class a value or variable belongs in the type() function is used, and to find out if an object belongs in a specific class, the isinstance() function is used.

In python numbers, the length of integers is boundless and can only be limited by the amount of available memory. Also, a floating-point number can maintain accuracy up to 15 decimal places. The presence of a decimal point shows the distinction between an integer and floating points. For example, 1 and 1.0 are the same in basic maths, but in Python, the former (1) is an integer, and the latter (1.0) is a floating number. Complex numbers are usually written in the following format, x + y; where x constitutes the real part of the equation, and the imaginary part is denoted by y.

PYTHON LIST:

A list refers to an ordered sequence of items. In python programming, list is one of the widely used datatypes owing to its relative flexibility. The items contained in a list do not have to share similarities in type to be on the list. Also, the process of declaring a list is quite easy. Items which are separated using commas and are contained within brackets []. The slicing operator [] is used in extracting a specific range of items or a single item from a list. In Python, index begins from the number 0. Lists can be mutable, meaning the value of the elements in a list is capable of being changed.

PYTHON TUPLE:

In Python, a tuple refers to an ordered sequence of items similar to list. The distinction, however, is that unlike lists, tuples are immutable. That is, once they have been created, the elements of a tuple cannot be changed or modified. Tuples are mainly used in place of lists to write-protect data as they are much faster and are incapable of changing dynamically. Tuples are defined with parentheses () where the items within are separated using commas. Moreover, even though a slicing operator [] can also be used to extract items, the values cannot be changed.

PYTHON SET

A set is a collection of special items which are not in any particular order. It is defined by values contained within braces {} and separated using commas. Like sets in basic mathematics, operations can be carried out on python sets such as the intersection and union of two sets.

Every set has a unique value, and since they are unordered, they do not require indexing. In this vein, the slicing operator [] cannot be used on sets.

PYTHON DICTIONARY

Like sets, python dictionary is a collection of key-value pairs in an unordered state. Dictionaries are used when there are vast volumes of data. Dictionaries are optimized to retrieve data. To do this, the key to retrieve a specific value must be known. In python programming, dictionaries exist as items being paired in the format key:value and contained within braces {}.

Moreover, the pair must not necessarily be of the same type. That is, key and value can be different types. In the pair, the key is used to retrieve a respective value, but it doesn't work vice versa.

CONVERSION BETWEEN DATA TYPES:

Conversion can be done from one data type to another using a several type conversion functions such as str(), float(), int() among others.

In converting from float to int, the value would be truncated to make it nearer to zero.

Only compatible values can be used in converting from and to string.

Conversion can also be done from one sequence to another sequence.

In converting to dictionary, every element must exist as a pair.

CHAPTER 7. FUNCTIONS AND MODULES IN PYTHON

In Python programming, functions refer to any group of related statements which perform a given activity. Functions are used in breaking down programs into smaller and modular bits. In that sense, functions are the key factors which make programs easier to manage and organize as they grow bigger over time. Functions are also helpful in avoiding repetition during coding and makes codes reusable.

- **The Syntax of Functions:**

The syntax of functions refers to the rules which govern the combination of characters that make up a function. These syntaxes include the following:

1. The keyword "def" highlights the beginning of every function header.
2. A function named is to identify it distinctly. The rules of making functions are the same as the rules which apply for writing identifiers in Python.
3. Parameters or arguments via which values are passed onto a function are optional in Python.
4. A colon sign (:) is used to highlight the end of every function header.

5. The optional documentation string known as do string is used to define the purpose of the function.
6. The body of a function is comprised of one or more valid statements in Python. The statements must all have a similar indentation level, (typically four spaces).
7. An optional return statement is included for returning a value from a function.

Below is a representation of the essential components of a function as described in the syntax.

def function_name(parameters):

'''docstring'''

statement(s)

- **How functions are called in Python:**

Once a function has been defined in Python, it is capable of being called from another function, a program, or the python prompt even. Calling a function is done by entering a function name with a proper parameter.

1. Docstring:

The docstring is the first string which comes after the function header. The docstring is short for documentation string and is used in explaining what a function does briefly. Although it is an optional part of a function, the documentation process is a good practice in programming. So, unless you have got an excellent memory which can recall what you had for breakfast on your first birthday, you should document your code at all times. In the example shown below, the docstring is used directly beneath the function header.

>>> greet("Amos")

Hello, Amos. Good morning!

Triple quotation marks are typically used when writing docstrings so they can extend to several lines. Such a string is inputted as the __doc__ attribute of the function. Take the example below.

You can run the following lines of code in a Python shell and see what it outputs:

1. >>> print(greet.__doc__)

2. This function greets to

3. the person passed into the

4. name parameter

2. The return statement:

The purpose of the return statement is to go back to the location from which it was called after exiting a function.

- **Syntax of return:**

This statement is able to hold expressions which have been evaluated and have their values returned. A function will return the Noneobject if the statement is without an expression, or its return statement is itself absent in the function. For instance:

1. >>> print(greet('Amos'))

2. Hello, Amos. Good morning!

3. None

In this case, the returned value is None.

CHAPTER 8. PYTHON FILE MANAGEMENT

File is a named memory location that is used to store and access data. Python manages file through a file object.

There are 4 basic file operations in Python:

1) opening a file
2) reading from a file
3) writing to a file
4) closing a file

Opening a File

The open() function creates a file object or handle that can be used to call other methods. You will use this function to open the file for reading, writing, or both.

syntax:

file object=open(filename [, access_mode][, buffering])

The filename refers to the file that you want to access.

The access mode is an optional parameter that will allow you to specify the access mode. There are two types of files that can be opened: a text file and binary file. There are several access modes for both files.

Modes for Accessing Text Files

r read mode (default); opens a file for reading

w write mode; creates a new file or overwrites existing one

r+ read and write mode

w+ read and write mode; creates a new file or overwrites an existing one

a append mode; adds data at end of file or creates new file if the file is non-existent

a+ read and append mode: appends data at end of file or creates new file if file is non-existent

x opens file for exclusive creation and fails if the file is already in existence

Modes for Accessing Binary Files

rb+ read and write

wb+ read and write mode; creates a new file or overwrite an existing file

ab+ read and append mode; adds data at end of file or create a new file if the file is non-existent

The buffering option lets users specify their preferred buffering style. When the value given is one, buffering is implemented as you access files. When the value exceeds one, buffering is carried out according to the specified buffer size. When a negative value is given, Python uses the system default.

To open a file in the default mode, the read mode:

```
f = open("diary.txt")
```

To open a file in write mode:

```
f = open("diary.txt",'w')
```

To read and write to a file in binary format:

```
f = open("reflection.bmp",'rb+')
```

Writing to a File

Before you can start writing to a file, you have to open the file with a file object:

```
>>> notes = open("myfile.txt", "w")
```

To start writing to a file, you will use the write method on the file object:

```
>>> notes.write("A file can be used to store important data.")
43
>>> notes.write("Files are objects that you can use in your program.")
51
```

Python returns the number of characters written on each line.

When you're done writing to a file, you have to close the file for proper processing and to avoid accidental erasure or alteration:

```
notes.close()
```

Reading a File

There are several ways to read a file:

- the readlines() method
- 'while' statement
- through an iterator

The readlines() Method

The readlines() method is a simple way to read and parse lines in a text file.

Using the file you created above, here are the steps:

Use a file object to open the file:

```
>>> notes = open("myfile.txt", "r")
```

Use the readlines() method on the file object to read each text line from the file. Create a variable that will store the text lines read:

```
>>> lines = notes.readlines()
```

Type the variable name on the Python prompt to access the contents of the file:

```
>>> lines
['A file can be used to store important data. Files are objects that you can use in your program.']
```

Close the file:

```
>>>notes.close()
```

Reading Files with a ‘while loop’

Reading files with a ‘while loop’ is a more efficient way to read larger files. To illustrate, build a new file with the open() function:

```
>>> message = open("newfile.txt", "w")
```

Write the following lines with a new line character (\n) at the end of each line:

```
>>> message.write("This file stores important messages.\n")
37

>>> message.write("Attendance is a must.\n")
22
```

Close the file:

```
>>>message.close()
```

To read the file using the readline method and the while loop:

```
# Open the linefile.txt on read only mode:
message = open('newfile.txt')

# Read the first line
textline = message.readline()

# keep reading line one at a time until file is empty
while textline:
    print(textline)
    textline = message.readline()
message.close()
```

When you run the above program, you will see the following line-by-line output on the Python shell:

```
This file stores important messages.


Attendance is a must.
```

Reading files with an iterator:

To read the newfile.txt with an iterator:

```
message = open('newfile.txt')

for x in iter(message):
    print(x)

message.close()
```

Appending Data to a File

To append data to an existing file, you need to open the file on append mode.

For example, to append data to newfile.txt, open the file and assign it to a new file handle:

```
>>> messages = open('newfile.txt', 'a')
```

Write a new line using the write method:

messages.write("Appending a line is as easy as writing a new line.")

50

Close the file:

```
>>> messages.close()
```

Use readlines() to view the updated newfile.txt:

```
>>>messages = open('newfile.txt')

>>> lines = messages.readlines()

>>> lines

['This file stores important messages.\n', 'Attendance is a must.\n', 'Appending a line is as easy as writing a new line.']
```

CHAPTER 9. INTRODUCTION TO OBJECT ORIENTED PROGRAMMING

Classes and objects are really important to how C# and other object-oriented programming languages will work. This is a pretty simple topic that you won't have trouble understanding, but this doesn't mean it's something you should ignore, it is actually very important that you should learn about it because it will help you learn how all of these work. This chapter will take the time to carefully look at how you can work with objects so that they will function the way they should in your code.

Classes and Objects

The first thing that we will spend our time talking about are the objects which are used in this programming language. Programming has changed a lot over the past few years, and this has changed how programmers create their new computer applications. The newest form of programming, known as 'OOP' or object-oriented programming, is the newest idea that most modern coding languages rely on to get the coding done. There are a lot of components that go with this, but it basically makes it easier to sort out and use the coding language.

Automation is the need of the current era, and with Python, you can automate tasks by writing test scripts, and Python surprises you here as well. You need a very little number of lines required to automate. This is because it supports lots of modules and tools, making stuff easy and instant.

Multipurpose

It is like the Swiss Army Knife, which would be used for many purposes. Python is not just a thing that deals with discipline but supports all sources of data like data from SQL or MongoDB. API of Python, which is called PySpark, is used to distribute computing. It has an inbuilt feature of service provision for natural language processing NLTK.

- Python also has many applications in the provision of services for internet protocol like XML, LSON, and HTML.

- Python enables you to draft a user interface for applications already made. To do this, there are tool kits available which are wxWidgets, Kivy which is for writing multi-touch applications and finally QT via PySide.

- It provides great applications for the scientific community like SciPy, which is a package for mathematics, engineering, and science. Pandas is a modeling and data analysis library.

- Python is extremely powerful when it comes to editing and works session recordings.

- Examples of What is OOP?

As a beginner, you may be curious as to what OOP means and how it's relevant to your coding. OOP is a style of coding that relies solely on objects to get the program to work. OOP will provide you with a model type that is based on how things would work in the real world and then you would use this idea and implement it in the codes that you are writing.

In some of the older coding languages, you had to concentrate on abstract ideas to help you to get the coding done. This may sound like a great idea, but it does make things more difficult in the long run. With OOP, you have to work with real objects, rather than these abstract ideas, which makes the coding so much easier. This is the approach that most modern programming languages take and it does make it much easier for the beginner to write their own codes, create their own program, and even solve some of their own problems they might encounter as they go about their programming.

Objects

In this section, we will spend some time working with objects to learn more about them. Programmers use digital objects to help represent the physical objects that they want to place inside of their code. While you are working with an OOP language, it is important to remember that these objects have more than a few characteristics that you should remember. These include:

State

These are the characteristics that will define the object. These can be general or specific.

Behavior

These are the characteristics that will declare all the actions that an object is capable of.

For us to understand exactly how all of this will work, we need to take a look at an example. Let's say that we are looking at a ball. The state of this object or the traits that define its characteristics are things like its color, what the ball is made out of, and the size. The behavior of that ball would refer to what that ball is capable of, such as bouncing, rolling, and so on and so forth.

When you are working on an OOP language, you can easily combine the technique and the information to process them as the same thing. The programming object will then match up to how it would behave or look when it is in the real world and then it will also hold onto the actions and the information until later.

Classes

Within this language, the 'classes' refer to what defines all the characteristics of the objects from above. These classes are in charge of giving you a model or a structure so that you can effectively define the nature of the object. These classes are often considered the foundation of OOP languages, and they will be linked closely to the object. Another thing to note is that each of the objects that you are using can also represent one specific class.

Let's take a look at how this works so that it makes a lot more sense to you. For example, we have a class that we named 'Toys' and while the object will be 'Ball.' In this sample, the ball is one instance of that 'Toy' class that you worked on. However, that the class will also define the state and the behavior of all the 'toys' that you add to the 'class' including the 'ball.'

Classes may sound complicated, and they will make the organization of your code a lot easier to handle, many people often see them as the basis of just about any program. The information they hold onto is meaningful for those who will take a look inside of the class so they can understand exactly what it is. For example, if you have a class that you named 'Toys,' the other users can access or look into the class and see that all the items or objects that were placed inside the code actually belong there.

They do not have to be exactly the same, but putting them together in the same class should make sense.

The classes function to define the behavior of an object, such as the kinds of actions you want that object to be capable of performing. The object will also have its own characteristics or attributes. You will see that the attributes appear as different variables in the body of the class while the behavior, on the other hand, is defined by the different methods that fall inside the class.

Let's take a look at how this works by examining the Toy class that we talked about before. When these are applied, you will get the size and the color as the attributes. To make this work, you will need to bring out and use the **move()** and the **stop()** methods.

How to use these classes in your code

We have already spent a little bit of time talking about classes and how you can get them to work inside of your code, but now we need to spend some more time looking at how they work within the program as a whole and how they are useful at changing what you can write out inside of the code. When you are working with the C# programming language, you need to define all of the classes with the help of the 'class' keyword to not only make sure that everything works but to also help make things clear and simple.

After you have started with the code and you typed in the word 'class,' this is when you should indicate the identifier that you would like to see with the variable and the methods that would help make it certain that all of this works. As for making sure that all of this would stay simple, there are specific parts that you need to use since you are working with this kind of code. The different parts that you need to add to the class when working in C# include:

Fields

These are any of the variables that belong to a particular data type.

Methods

You can use these methods to manipulate the data.

Properties

In this programming language, the properties are what will enhance how well the fields work. The property will provide some extra management abilities for the information and give it to the fields.

At this point, it will probably be easier if you take a look at how you can work with making classes and how to make sure that they do exactly what you would like. We will now have a look at an example of how this code will work and the different theories that have been going on with it. In this example, we will use 'book' as the name of the class and then it will have the properties of 'size' and 'type.'

CHAPTER 10. REAL WORLD EXAMPLES OF PYTHON

One might argue that the era of Python was just 2017 when it witnessed some great rise in the popularity and growth across the world. The recent However, according to statistics and data, the recent rise in the growth of Python could not be ignored.

However, why do you think it will keep on attaining the rise in the expansion and in size? To answer the question, we dive into the market data and the scale of Python adoption and acquisition by corporations and companies around the world.

SO the reason behind the popularity of Python is one and simple. It will be as popular and widely used five years from now as it was five years ago. This is a big statement and to prove this, we need to see in detail what makes Python so special for these developers and programmers.

Years ago, when Python came into the market, people believed it would be dead within months of inception. In face when Larry Wall who is also the founder and brain behind programing language Perl was delivering his third annual state of Pearl Opinion said that there are some programming languages out there in the market that are C++, Java, Perl, Visual Basics, Javascript and in the last Python. Back then, the leading language for programming was C++ and Perl was on the third number in the market. Python had very low demand and was not included among the PLs that could grow.

However, in the years to follow, Python grew with tremendous speed and outshined Perl as well. According to Stack Overflow, the visitor volume to question and enquire about Python increased more rapidly than Perl.

Following are the reasons behind the rise and super demand for Python among developers.

Data Science

This is one of the most adored languages among data scientists, unlike R and C++. SO the current era is the era of big data, and since Python supports large sets of libraries, internet, and prototypes, Python is the best and fully suited language for the operations. PyMySQL, PyBrain, and NumPy are the reason why is Python so extensively demanded. In addition, integrations and programming are the things a programmer has to deal in everyday life, and this is the reason behind the huge demand for Python as well because it provides easy integration even of existing apps or sites to other programming languages. This makes it future-oriented and scalable.

Machine Learning

In the industry these days, artificial intelligence and machine learning have created a huge buzz with every industry investing in the areas to maximize their revenue and cut costs. This is not really possible without thc induction of Python. It is actually an interpreted language, and its use makes it elucidated enough to be interpreted by machines and to be understood by the hardware. The growth of ML has been on the rise in the last few years, and I think this is also one of the reasons why Python has witnessed a surge in its demand.

Applications in Web Development

According to data, Python is chosen by two out of three developers who in the start worked with OHO, and this is an achievement. The rising trend of Python in the last couple of years shows that it seems like the best alternative. It offers Flask and Django, which makes the process of web development easy and quick. It is due to these reasons and features that leading tech giants like Google, Facebook, Instagram, etc. have been using it for long. Uber and Google use it for its algorithms. In addition, it is super simple, and this is the reason why it is easy to work with and adaptable.

Automation

software development applications are SCons, which is for build control, Roundup, and Trace, which are for bug tracking and project management. For IDE integrated development environments, Roster is used.

- The most important stuff related to Python is that it provides special applications for education.

- Its applications in business include Tryton, which is a 3-tier and advanced level application platform. Another management software called Odoocomes with a huge deal of business applications. This actually makes Python an all-rounder.

- For network programming, we have Twisted Python which provides a platform and framework for the network programming that is asynchronous. It has a simple socket interface.

- We all know that the gaming industry is evolving with great potential and ability to create replicated amount of revenue.

The applications of Python for gaming is very safe to use and have been pretty much and widely used. PyGame and PyKyra are bi-development frameworks for games. There is also a variety of 3D rendering options in the libraries.

- Moreover, we have applications which interest the developers to a huge extent and are used widely. We have applications that are console-based, applications for robotics, machine learning and web scraping and scripting and whatnot.

These are the main reason why Python is the best fit in the industry from the point of view of a developer.

According to a report of myTectra, the jobs which were posted in Naukri from 2014 to 2017 have been monitored. The trend of Python jobs is compared to the world's number one language showing different results.

THINGS WE CAN DO IN PYTHON

In this Chapter, we will discuss many things that you can do in Python. Some of the things we can do in Python include the comments, reading and writing, files and integers, strings, and variables. We are sure that after reading this the book, you will be able to create the program that will run effectively. Due to the interactive and descriptive nature of the Python, a beginner can handle many things using it. Therefore, this chapter will discuss some aspects and comments in Python to help you get started. You can make amazing codes in a short time using the Python programming language.

Comment

A comment, in the Python programming, starts with the # sign. This continues until the programmer gets to the end of the line. A good example is;

This is a comment

Print (hello, thanks for contacting us)

It instructs your computer to print “hello, thanks for contacting us”. In fact, the Python interpreter ignores all the comments. As a programmer, however, you should not leave a comment after every line. You can put in a comment when you need to explain something. Since long comments are not supported by Python, it is important to use short and descriptive comments to avoid them going across the lines.

READING AND WRITING

You will realize that some program requests specific information or show the text on the screen. Sometimes we start the program code by informing the readers about our programs. To make things look easy for the other coders, it is important to give it the name or title that is simple and descriptive.

As a programmer, you can use a string literal that comprises the print function to get the right data. String literal is a line of the text surrounded by the quotes. They can be either double or single quotes. Although the type of quotes a programmer use matters less, the programmer must end with the quotes that he/she has used at the beginning of the phrase. You can command your computer to display a phrase or a word on the screen by just doing as discussed above.

Files

Apart from using the print function to obtain a string when printing on the screen, it can be used to write something onto the file. First, you will have to open up the myfile.txt and write on it before assigning it the myfile which is a variable. Once you have completed the first step, you will have to assign "w" in the new line to tell the program that you will only write or make changes after the file has opened. It is not mandatory to use print function; just use the right methods like read method.

Read method is used to open specific files to help you read the available data. You can use this option to open a specific file. Generally, the read method helps the programmers to read the contents into variable data, making it easy for them to open the program they would like to read.

Integers

Always make sure that the integers are kept as whole numbers if you are using them. They can be negative or positive only if there are no decimals. However, if your number has a decimal point, use it as a floating number. Python will automatically display such integers in the screen.

Moreover, you cannot place one number next to others if you are using the integers because Python is a strongly typed language; thus it will not recognize them when you use them together. However, you put both the number and the string together by making sure you turn the number into a string first before going to the next steps.

TRIPLE QUOTES

After reading and understanding both the single and double quotes, it is now a time to look at the triple quotes. The triple quotes are used to define the literal that spans many lines. You can use three singles, double, or single when defining an authentic.

Strings

Although a string is seen as a complicated thing to many beginners, it is a term used by the programmers when referring to a sequence of characters and works just like a list. A string contains more functionality which is specific than a list. You will find it challenging to format the strings when writing out the code because some messages will not be fixed easily due to its functionality. String formatting is the only way to go away within such a situation.

ESCAPE SEQUENCES

They are used to donate special characters which are hard to type on the keyboard or those that can be reserved to avoid confusion that may occur in programming.

OPERATOR PRECEDENCE

It will help you to track what you are doing in Python. In fact, it makes things easy when ordering the operation to receive the right information. So, take enough time to understand how the operator precedence works to avoid confusion.

Variables

Variables refer to the labels donated somewhere in the computer memory to store something like holding values and numbers. In the programming typed statistically, the variables have predetermined values. However, Python enables you to use one variable to store many different types. For example, in the calculator, variables are like memory function to hold values which can be retrieved in case you need them later. The variables can only be erased if you store them in the newer value. You will have to name the variable and ensure it has an integer value.

Moreover, the programmer can define a variable in Python by providing the label value. For instance, a programmer can name a variable count and even make it an integer of one, and this can be written as; count=1. It allows you to assign the same name to the variable, and in fact, the Python interpreter cannot read through the information if you are trying to access values in the undefined variable. It will display a message showing syntax error. Also, Python provides you with the opportunity of defining different variables in one line even though this not a good according to our experience.

THE SCOPE OF A VARIABLE

It is not easy to access everything in Python, and there will be differences in the length of the variables. However, the way we define the variable plays a vital role in determining the location and the duration of accessing the variables. The part of the program that allows you to access the variable is called the Scope while the time taken for accessing the variable is a lifetime.

Global variables refer to the variables defined in the primary file body. These variables are visible throughout the file and also in the file that imports specific data. As such, these variables cause a long-term impact which you may notice when working on your program. This is the reason why it is not good to use global variables in the Python program. We advise programmers to add stuff into the global namespace only if they plan to use them internationally. A local variable is a variable defined within another variable. You can access local variables from the region they are assigned. Also, the variables are available in the specific parts of the program.

MODIFYING VALUES

For many programming languages, it is easy for an individual to define a particular variable whose values have been set. The values which cannot be modified or changed, in the programming language, are called constants. Although this kind of restrictions is not allowed in Python, there are used to ensure some variables are marked indicating that no one should change those values. You must write the name in capital letters, separated with underscores. A good example is shown below.

NUMBER_OF_HOURS_IN_A_DAY=24

It is not mandatory to put the correct number at the end. Since Python programming does not keep tracking and has no rules for inserting the correct value at the end, you are free and allowed to say, for example, that they are 25 hours in a day. However, it is important to put the correct value for other coders to use in case they want.

Modifying values is essential in your string as it allows a programmer to change the maximum number in the future. Therefore, understanding the working of the string in the program contributes a lot to the success of your program. One has to learn and know where to store the values, the rules governing each value, and how to make them perform well in a specific area.

THE ASSIGNMENT OPERATOR

Although discussed in this book earlier, we had not given it the specific name. It refers to an equal sign (=). You will be using the assignment operator to assign values to the variable located at the left side on the right of the statement. However, you must evaluate if the value on the right side is an arithmetic expression. Note that the assignment operator is not a mathematical sign in the programming because, in programming, we are allowed to add all types of things and make them look like they are equivalent to a certain number. This sign is used to show that those items can be changed or turned into the part on the other side.

CHAPTER 11. EXAMPLES OF CODING

LOOPS

Loops are generally utilized whenever one computer system is used when there is a program needed to repeat processes more than once. This particular process is referred to as 'iteration' and there will end up being 1 loop that is 'for' and the other is called a 'while' loop in Python. The first image is a representation of the 'for' loop and the 2nd image is the easiest of the two and is the 'while' loop.

WORKING AND STRINGS

Strings as part of python, frequently tend to be a conterminous collection of recognizable possibility delimited through a line or possibly multiple quotes. Python wouldn't possess any kind of distinct information range for a recognizable possibility; therefore, they frequently tend to be portrayed as the lone recognizable string.

Creating strings

It is essentially the string of recognizable possibility; the string takes place to be as part of the fact. The recognizable takes place to be as part of the character. For example, the English language has 26 recognizable possibilities.

Computer systems do not contend with mere possibility. They contend with actual numbers (with decimal points included). It is quite possibly an option, however, that you may not notice any recognizable options on your display screen inside. It takes place to be as part of the fact actually store and analyzed as a series and combinations of zeros (o) and ones (1).

This conversion process recognizable to the number takes place to be a part of fact called encoding. The reverse process takes place to be as part of the fact called decoding. ASCII and Unicode frequently tend to be more of the favored among users and especially beginners, as it relates to Python strings, which tend to take place in a hidden bit of Unicode that remains recognizable.

Unicode was originally coded to include all things considered and bring consistency as a major aspect of encoding. You can take in additional about Unicode from here.

Strings as a Python Feature:

Strings can be made through encasing unmistakable probability inside singular quotation marks or multiple quotes. It is up to you what your desired outcome will be. For the most part, Python is typically used to be a representation of multiple strings and doc-strings.

When you run the program, your specific output will be: If ran and executed properly.

There are numerous tasks that can be performed with the string that makes it a standout amongst the most utilized types of data in Python.

Link of Two or More Strings - Joining of at least two strings into a solitary one is called "concatenation".

The "+" function allows you to compose 2 string literals together and links them.

The " *" function can bc utilizcd to rehash the string for a set number of repetitions.

CHAPTER 12. QUIZ AND WORKBOOK

To optimize your use of the Python program as a beginner, here are significant pointers that can help your learning activity become fruitful.

1. Be positive. Anything new can be daunting – especially a 'foreign' language. Think about learning Korean, Chinese or Spanish, and you won't even want to start. But optimism can make you change your mind. As Master Yoda from "Star Wars' said: "Do, there is no try." Believe that you can do it, and you can. Think about all the benefits you can derive from what you will learn.
2. Python is an extensive program; continue learning. What we have discussed here is only the tip of the iceberg. There are still thousands of complex information about Python that you can learn.
3. If you want to obtain several values from a list, use the 'slice' function, instead of using the index. This is because the 'index' can provide you a single value only.
4. Assign only integer values to indices. Other number forms are not recognized by Python. Keep in mind that index values start from zero (0).
5. Remember to use the 'help' function whenever necessary. Explore the 'help' function, when in doubt on what to do. A little help from Python can go a long way.
6. Python programming is a dynamic language. Thus, you can experiment and come up with a code of your own to contribute towards its advancement.

7. There are some differences among the Python versions. But don't fret, the program itself has built-in modules and functions that can assist you in solving the problems you can encounter.

8. The interactive shell can promptly return results. That's why it's preferable to open a 'New File' first, before creating your statement. But if you're sure of your code, then, go ahead, and use the interactive shell directly.

9. Separate your multiple statements, in a single line, with semicolons. This is easier and more sensible.

10. The three 'greater than' signs (>>>) or arrows is a prompt from the interactive shell. You can explore their functionality as you create your statements.

11. The Python interpreter can act as a calculator. Using your interactive shell, you can compute math problems quickly – and continuously. No sweat!

12. The # symbol indicates that the statement is a comment. The # sign is placed before the comment, and after the Python statement, so Python won't mistake it as part of the statement or code.

13. Use the reverse or back slash (\ ) to escape a single quote, or double quotes. Examples of these are contracted words, such as 'don't, "won't", 'aren't'. When using them in Python, they will appear this way: 'don\'t', "won\'t", 'aren\'t'.

14. A short cut in joining two literal strings (strings literal) is to put them beside each other and

enclose each in quotes. Example: 'Clinical' 'Chemistry'. This will give: ClinicalChemistry.

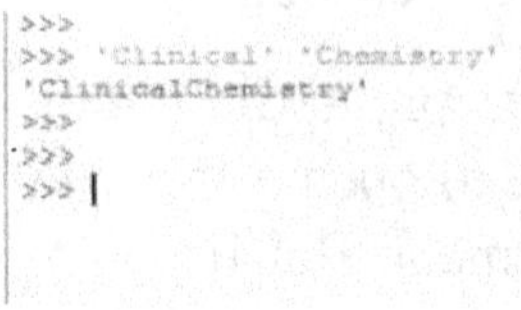

```
>>>
>>> 'Clinical' 'Chemistry'
'ClinicalChemistry'
>>>
>>>
>>> |
```

15. For modifying immutable data, create a new file. These immutable data include strings, numbers, frozen set, bytes and Tuples. By creating a new file, you can modify, add and remove items from your immutable data.

QUIZ

1. Why do you think multi-line statements are necessary we can simply write a single line, and the program statement will run just fine?

2. List the variable scope types?

3. Start IDLE.

Navigate to the File menu and click New Window.

Type the following:

```
food=['omelet', 'fish','rice']
for j in range(len(food)):
  print("I prefer", food[j])
```

ANSWERS

1. Multi-line statements can help improve formatting/readability of the entire program. Remember, when writing a program always assume that it is other people who will use and maintain it without your input.

2. The following are the scope types:

i. Scope containing local names, current function.

ii. Scope containing global names, the scope of the module.

iii. Scope containing built-in names of the outermost scope.

3. The output of this program will be:

I prefer omelet

I prefer fish

I prefer jazz

CHAPTER 13. BONUS: WORKBOOK

You have already seen that Python can sometimes be rather difficult to operate. But, with a few tips and tricks, you can make Python that much easier for you to use so that you do not have to worry so much about something not making sense in your code.

Strings

As started earlier, triple quotes are going to be the easiest way that you are going to be able to set the definition of a string.

Str.join ( ) can be used when you are using string concentration.

The only time that you are going to use string concentration is when your string is a thousand characters or more.

Example

Print "peanut butter" + "jelly" + "peanut butter" #this type of coding should not ever be done!

Print " " join(["peanut butter" , "jelly" , "and" , "peanut butter"]) #while it does not seem like it, this is going to be more efficient for your code in Python. You may also notice that this is a Python idiom that is used often.

Print "%s %s %s %s %s ("peanut butter," "jelly," "and," "peanut butter") #this is also a method that is pythonic as well as an example for string concentration.

Modules that are used in C

Some modules will actually be faster when the program is running because of the language that they are written in.

The C language is going to be identical to the other languages that are used in Python. The biggest difference is that it is going to be faster because of the implementations that Python uses. Module behavior will end up being different when C is being used, but the differences are not going to be noticed by the user.

C versions are going to be used in more versions of Python than any other language.

Modules will be optimized but only in the event that they are available with the version of Python that you are using.

cProfile is going to be what is going to be used in Python 3.4.

Importation

In the C version of Python, you are going to notice the name of the modules that you use are going to begin with the letter c so that it can be set aside as being written in a different language.

When you are importing this file, you are not going to use the c for the import process.

The reason that you are going to forget the c is because you are going to be using the original Python version. The code will be converted to C in the program.

Example

Import cName as Name

Except Import error for this file.

Import Name

Examples

Python 2.x is going to carry out commands in C over a thousand times faster than if you were to use a different method.

In Python 2.x you are also going to add a c to the string function.

Python 3 is going to replace that c with an io

A cprofile in Python is going to have overhead added to it and that is why it is going to be the one that is recommended for you to use.

If you are using a version of Python that is 3.3 or higher the celementtree is going to be the same as the element tree. Element tree ends up being about twenty times faster and is going to consume less memory than other methods that you have to choose from. As mentioned, if you have version 3.3 then it is going to be done by the program automatically since it is a faster method of keeping the program going.

Comprehension and generators

Smaller loops should be used with a generated expression or through the use of list comprehension.

Comprehension can be also make for loops go faster so that you do not have to worry about making a mistake.

A dictionary is going to be a section of the program that is going to contain files that are going to help the program run the code that you are wanting to be run.

The files that are in the directory is usually going to be used for making sure that all the rules for the loop that you are making are being followed. If conditions are going to make the search through the directory more narrow so that it goes faster.

Expressions that have been generated can be used with a multitude of lists as long as you use the zip function.

Data type

To figure which data type you should use, you are going to need to look at the application and determine how it is going to run with each data type.

In comparing two lists to see if there is anything similar between the two of them, you are going to have to go through each element individually, but this is going to take up too much of your time and you may end up forgetting what you are trying to do.

Instead of going through the list you are going to use a function that is going to go through the list for you and find what each list has in common.

This method should only be used on smaller lists. There is another method that you can use for lists that have more entries so that it is more efficient and less time consuming.

A set is going to help speed up the process when you are using it as a function.

A dictionary is not going to be recommended when you are using a set since sets are mutable, but a tuple is going to be the perfect choice for you.

Dictionaries that have to be used are going to convert your objects into the tuple or list so that you can do the proper operation so that it can be converted back to the form that it should be in for the program.

Methods such as this are going to be faster than attempting to duplicate the string.

Other

Logging and database access is going to be handled by a decorator.

There is no function that has been placed into Python as of yet that is going to enable you to make a list smaller as you work on it. However, you can use a recursive function which is going to do the same thing, but it is going to do it when you have finished creating your list.

A GUI button has been placed in Python that was originally based off of the TcI's Tk. This is going to give you access to things that are in Python 4 and Python 3 that you do not have access to in other versions of Python.

Swapping two numbers

Thanks to Python, there is a way that you can switch the place of two numbers that are all in one line.

Example

Z, t = 15, 5

Print (z, t)

Z, t – t, z

Print (z, t)

First (15, 5)

Second (5, 15)

This function actually makes a new tuple while the previous one is left unreferenced.

After the new tuple is created, it is going to be flagged by the program because of the variables that have been switched.

Comparison operators

Comparison operators can be aggregated so that you can chain the two operators together.

Example

Z = 5

Result = 2 < z < 25

Print (result)

#this statement is true

Result = 1 > z <= 4

Print (result)

#this statement is false

Ternary operators and conditional assignments

A ternary operator is going to be the short way of writing out an if else statement

Syntax

[on_true] if [expression] else [on_false]

Example

Z = 15 if (t == 5) else 50

Class objects can also use ternary operators

Example

Z = (classB if y == 2 else classD)(param4, param7)

When the number of parameters has been set, ternary operators can be used to evaluate the smaller numbers that are in the expression

Example

Def small(d, r, g) :

Return d if d <= r and d <= g else (r if r <= d and r <= g else g)

Print(small(2, 5, 2))

Print(small(6, 3, 3))

```
Print(small( 3, 3, 4))

Print(small(9, 8, 7))
```

Output

```
2,3,4,5,6,7,8,9
```

List comprehension can use ternary operators as well.

Multi-line strings

Backslashes are going to be used with the C language .

Example

```
multiStr = “choose * from one of the statements \
depending on placement_id < 6”
print(multiStr)
```

#you are going to choose one from the statements that are listed where the placement_id is 6

Triple quotes work just as well

multiStr = “””choose * from one of the statements \

depending on placement_id < 6”””

print(multiStr)

#you are going to choose one from the statements that are listed where the placement_id is 6

When using triple quotes, the indentation is going to be a problem because the quotes are going to get in the way of the indentation. Trying to place our own indentations is going to result in whitespaces.

So, to correct this, the string is going to be split up and there are going to be parentheses that will enclose the entire code.

Example

multiStr = (“ choose * from one of the statements”

“where placement_id < 6”

“select by number”)

Print (multiStr)

#you are going to select from the multiple rows available where the placement_id is < 6 and selected by number.

Elements placed in a list with new variables

Lists can be used with a great number of variables.

The number of variables that are in your list should never go past the number of elements that are in your list

Example

Listest = [5, 8 2]

Z, u, I = listest

Print (z, u, I)

#The numbers are going to be 5, 8, 5

Interactive operators

Expressions can be tested with a temporary name.

The underscore is going to take the place of the expression that you are wanting to test so that you are not testing the actual expression and potentially messing up your code.

Example

3 + 5

8

_

8

Print _

8

Set comprehension and dictionaries

Set comprehension and dictionaries are going to work just like list comprehension does.

Example

```
Dicttest = { z: z* z for z in xrange ( 5) }
Settest = { z * 8 for z in x range ( 5) }

Print (settest)
Print( dicttest)

#set ( [ 0, 5, 10, 15, 20])
```

When you are using < : > there is going to be a difference from just the regular commas.

Code that is run in Python 3 is going to replace the xrange with just the normal word of range.

We are happy that you have made up your mind to start the journey of mastering Python. One of the most common questions that new learners want to know is how to learn a given language.

Well, the first step in becoming a master in Python programming is to ensure that you know how to learn. Knowing how to learn is a vital skill in computer programming.

So why is it important for you to know how to learn? Simply put: language changes, new libraries are created, and new tools are released. Thus, if you know how to learn, it will be important to help you remain at par with these changes and become a successful developer.

This chapter will provide you with tips that will help you kick start your journey of becoming a master in python programming.

HOW TO MAKE NEW CONCEPTS STICK

Practice coding daily

Consistency is a key element when trying to learn anything new. Whether you want to learn how to drive a car, how to cook pizza, or even play basketball, you must be consistent. And learning a new language isn't an exception. You may not believe it but the muscle memory plays a huge role in programming. By coding daily, you will be boosting that muscle memory. Although this can be difficult in the first few weeks, you should try and begin with 25 minutes per day, and slowly increase the length of time each day.

Write something down

Concepts will not stick in your brain just by staring at them; you must have a pen and a notebook to take notes. Research indicates that taking notes by hand increases the level of retention. If you want to become a full-time Python developer, then you must take notes, and write down some lines of code.

Once you begin to work on small programs, writing by hand can assist you to know how to plan your code before you shift to the computer. This will help you save a lot of time, especially if you can write out the type of functions, variables, and classes you will need.

Don't be dull but be active

Whether you are learning how to debug an application or learning about Python lists, the Python shell should be your favorite tool. Use it to test out some Python codes and concept.

Give yourself a break

You know that work without play makes Jack a dull boy, so take breaks and allow the concepts to sink. Take a break of 25 minutes, then come back and resume your learning process. Breaks ensure that you have an efficient study session, especially when you are learning new information.

Breaks will be crucial when you start to debug your program. If you get a bug and you can't tell how to fix it, a break could answer to your problem. Step away from your computer and refresh yourself.

Maybe it could be a missing quotation mark that is preventing your program from running, and that break will make a difference.

Love to fix bugs

When it comes to hitting bugs, this is one thing that you will never miss if you begin to write advanced Python programs. Running into bugs is something that happens to everyone who codes. It doesn't matter which language you are using. Don't let bugs get the better of you. So you need to embrace any moment you encounter a bug and think of yourself as a master of solving bugs.

When you start to debug, ensure that you have a methodological strategy to assist you in identifying where things are going wrong. Scanning through your code by following the steps in which the program is implemented is a great way to debug. Once you identify the problem, then you can think of how to solve it.

Work with others

Surround yourself with people who are learning

While coding can appear as a solitary task, it really works well when you collaborate with others. It is very crucial that when you are learning how to program in Python that you have friends who are in the same boat as you. This will give you room to share amongst yourselves the tricks to help in learning.

Don't be scared if you don't have anyone that you can collaborate with. In fact, there are many ways to meet like-minded developers passionate about Python development. You can go to local events and peer to peer learning community for Python lovers and Meetups.

Teach

The best way to master something is to teach others. This is true when you are learning Python. There are different ways you can do this. For example, you can create blog posts that describe newly learned concepts, record videos where you explain something, or even talk to yourself. Each of these methods will solidify your knowledge and reveal any gaps in your understanding.

Try out pair programming

In this approach, two programmers work in a single workstation to finish a task. The two developers then switch tasks. One writes the code and the other one guides the process and reviews the code as it is being written. Switch tasks often to experience the benefit of both sides.

This technique has many advantages. For instance, you get the chance to have another person review your code and also see how the other person could be thinking about the problem. By getting exposed to numerous ideas and approaches of thinking will help you know how to create solutions to problems using Python.

Ask smart questions

You may have heard someone say that there is no bad question but in programming, it is possible to ask a bad question. When asking questions from someone who has very little knowledge or context of the problem you want to solve, it is advised to follow this format:

G: Give context on the area you want to solve.

O: Outline everything you have attempted to fix

O: Offer the best guess of what the problem could be.

D: Demonstrate what is happening

Asking a good question can save a lot of time. If you skip any of the following steps can lead to conflict because of the back-and-forth conversations. As a newbie, you want to ensure that you only ask good questions so that you can learn how to express your thought process. Also, the people who help you can be happy to assist you again.

Create something

Above all, you only learn by doing. Doing exercises will help you make important steps but building something will take you far.

Build anything

For new beginners, there are always small exercises that will boost your confidence in Python. Once you have a solid foundation on basic data structures, writing classes, and object-oriented programming, then you can begin to build something.

What you build is not as important as the method you use. The path of the building is what will help you learn the most. You can only learn a lot from reading Python books, articles, and courses.

Most of your learning will originate from developing something. The problems you will solve will help you learn a lot.

If you find it hard to come up with a python practice project to work on, you can get started with the following:

Dice roll simulator.

Number guessing game.

Simple calculator.

Bitcoin price notification system

Participate in open source programs

In the open source system, you can access the source code of a software, and anyone can take part. Python has a lot of open-source projects that you can decide to contribute. Besides that, many companies post open-source projects. In other words, you can contribute to the code written and generated by engineers working in some of these companies.

CONCLUSION

The next step is to go on to more complicated topics. You've started the long and often arduous journey of programming in this book. And the best thing about it? There's no finite end point. There's never going to be a point in programming where you say enough is enough, or where you reach some kind of "peak"in your knowledge. Well, technically speaking, maybe, but only if you quit trying will you have hit a peak.

Programming is one of the most liberating tasks known to man, because it's the ultimate art form. It's the most interactive art form too. When you program, what you're doing is literally talking to the computer, and thereby making the computer talk to the user. Every single program you make is an extension of the effort that you put into it and the time and the code that you've dedicated to it.

Programming, too, is not easy. In fact, it's rather difficult. And there are topics that are sadly too esoteric to cover in this book. For example, we didn't get to the bulk of file operations, nor did we get to things like object-oriented programming. But I hope what I've given you is a very solid foundational understanding of Python so that you can better service **yourself** to learn about these things.

My goal here wasn't explicitly to teach you **Python** or object-oriented programming or any of that: my goal was to teach you the **computer**. The way it thinks, and the way programs are written. Anybody can learn Python keywords. But to learn to program, and to write solid effective code regardless of which programming language that you're using, that's another skill entirely.

PYTHON FOR DATA SCIENCE

The Practical Beginner's Guide to Learn Python Data Science in One Day Step-By-Step (#2020 updated version | Effective Computer Programming)

Steve Tudor

Legal & Disclaimer

The information contained in this book and its contents is not designed to replace or take the place of any form of medical or professional advice; and is not meant to replace the need for independent medical, financial, legal or other professional advice or services, as may be required. The content and information in this book has been provided for educational and entertainment purposes only.

The content and information contained in this book has been compiled from sources deemed reliable, and it is accurate to the best of the Author's knowledge, information and belief. However, the Author cannot guarantee its accuracy and validity and cannot be held liable for any errors and/or omissions. Further, changes are periodically made to this book as and when needed. Where appropriate and/or necessary, you must consult a professional (including but not limited to your doctor, attorney, financial advisor or such other professional advisor) before using any of the suggested remedies, techniques, or information in this book.

Upon using the contents and information contained in this book, you agree to hold harmless the Author from and against any damages, costs, and expenses, including any legal fees potentially resulting from the application of any of the information provided by this book. This disclaimer applies to any loss, damages or injury caused by the use and application, whether directly or indirectly, of any advice or information presented, whether for breach of contract, tort, negligence, personal injury, criminal intent, or under any other cause of action.

You agree to accept all risks of using the information presented inside this book.

You agree that by continuing to read this book, where appropriate and/or necessary, you shall consult a professional (including but not limited to your doctor, attorney, or financial advisor or such other advisor as needed) before using any of the suggested remedies, techniques, or information in this book.

Introduction

There are different tools that can be used for data analysis. Examples of these include ***SAS*** programming, ***Hadoop***, ***R*** programming, ***SQL***, ***Python***, and others. Amongst these tools, Python has a very unique feature as it is a general feature programming language whose syntax is easy to grasp.

Python has been in existence for a long time and it has been used in many industries like oil, scientific computing, gas, physics, finance, signal processing, and many others. It has been used for the development of applications like ***YouTube*** and it has played a great role in powering the internal infrastructure of ***Google***.

Python is a powerful tool for data science due to its flexibility and being open source. It is well known for its many libraries that can be used for data manipulation Examples of such libraries include ***Pandas***, ***Scikit-Learn***, ***TensorFlow***, ***PyTorch***, ***NumPy***, ***Scipy***, and ***PyBrain***. Alongside these, there is the ***Cython library*** that helps in converting Python code to run in a C environment to reduce runtime, ***PyMySQL*** that helps in connecting to ***MySQL databases***, extracting data and executing queries.

Data analysis goes hand-in-hand with data visualization. Python has made a number of improvements to overtake its competitor, R, in data visualization. We now have APIs like ***Plotly*** and libraries like ***Matplotlib***, ***Pygal***, ***ggplot***, ***NetworkX***, and others for data visualization. Python can also be integrated with other data visualization tools like Tableau and ***Qlikview*** using ***TabPy*** and ***win32com*** respectively.

Currently, ***Hadoop*** is the largest platform for data analysis. Python is compatible with Hadoop, which has made it a widely adopted language for data analysis. The ***PyDoop*** API provides us with access to HDFS API to connect our program to the HDFS installation. After that, we can write, read and get information on directories, files as well as global file system properties. PyDoop also provides us with the ***MapReduce API*** to help us in solving complex problems with little programming.

Part 1 : FUNDAMENTALS OF DATA SCIENCE

Chapter 1. what is data science

Data Science is an art. It is not a concept that one can teach a computer. Data analysts use different tools to achieve their tasks, right from linear regression to classification trees. Even though all these tools are known to the computer, it is the role of the data analyst to figure out a way in which he or she can gather all the tools and integrate them to data to

develop the correct answer to a question.

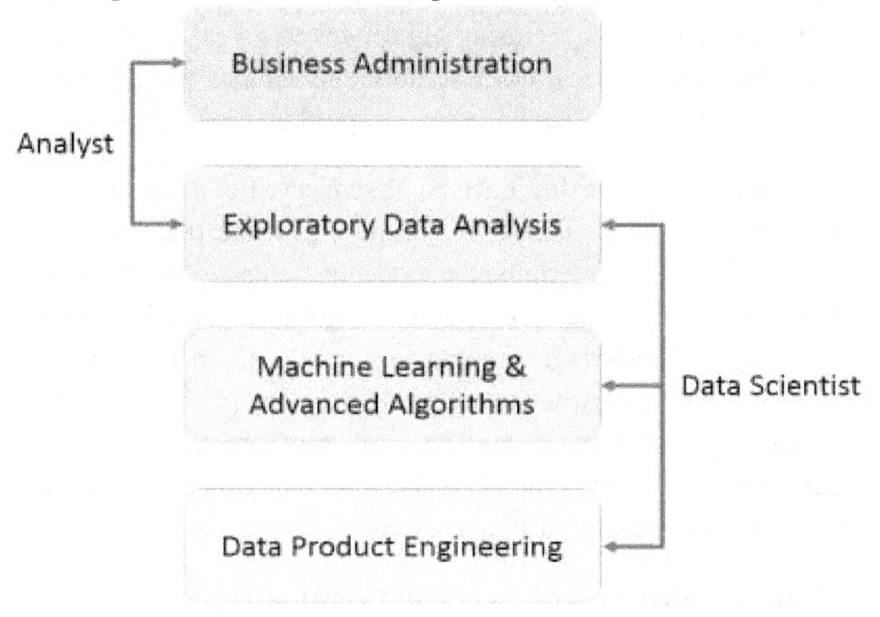

The figure above shows that a Data Analyst explains whatever is happening by processing the history of the data. On the other hand, a A Data Scientist looks at the data from different perspectives and angles.

Therefore, Data Science helps an individual predict and make decisions by taking advantage of prescriptive analytics, machine learning, and predictive causal analytics.

- **Prescriptive Analytics.** If you need a model that has the intelligence and capability to make its own decisions, then prescriptive analytics is the best to use.

This new field delivers advice; it doesn't just predict, but it also recommends different prescribed actions and related outcomes. Data that is collected by the vehicle is used to train cars. You can further mine this data by using algorithms to reveal intelligence. This will allow your car to make decisions such as when to turn, which path to take, as well as when to speed up or slow down.

- **Machine Learning for Pattern Discovery.** Let's say that you don't have resources that you can apply to make predictions; it will require you to determine the hidden patterns in the data set to predict correctly. The most popular algorithm used in pattern discovery is Clustering. Assume that you work in a telephone company, and you want to determine a network by installing towers in the region. Therefore, you may use the clustering technique to determine the tower location that will make sure all users have the maximum signal strength.

- **Make Predictions with Machine Learning.** If you can predict the future trend of a company, then Machine Learning algorithms are the best to go with. This falls under supervised learning; it is called supervised because data is already present that you can use to train machines.

Data Science and Discovery of Data Insight

The main aspect of Data Science is to discover findings from data. It involves unearthing hidden insight that can allow companies to make smart business decisions. For example:

- **Highlighting key customer segments inside its base as well as special shopping behaviors in the segments. This directs messages to different market audiences.**
- **Netflix extracts data from movie viewing patterns to find out what drives user interest and uses it to make decisions.**

- **Proctor and Gamble make use of time series models to understand future demand. This allows a person to plan for production levels.**

But how do Data Scientists extract data insights? If you ever asked yourself this question, the answer is: it begins with data exploration. When faced with a difficult problem, Data Scientists become curious. They attempt to find leads and understand characteristics within the data. To achieve this, an individual must have a higher level of creativity.

Besides, they may choose to use quantitative techniques to move deeper. Some examples are time series forecasting, inferential models segmentation analysis, synthetic control experiments, and many more. The aim is to put together a forensic view of what the data means. Hence, data-driven insight is the key in delivering strategic guidance. In other words, the role of Data Scientists is to guide business stakeholders so that they can learn how to respond to findings.

Chapter 2. different areas of application

While there is a lot that you can do with data science, you must remember that it is mainly just a tool that you use in business. If you know how to use it properly and you make sure to stay efficient with it, data science can be a great tool that helps limit your risk and even make you more money. However, if you do not use it properly, it could easily cause a lot more harm to your business than it does good.

It is easy to become captivated with all of the possibilities that can come with data science. But if your business can't afford it or if you just try to use it without the right experience or knowledge, then you will end up costing your business a lot of money. Make sure that the data science team and the management team become are aware of some crucial points along the way.

What management needs to know

To get as much out of the wealth of data that a business has, and information on the Internet, management must think of the data analytically. If management is not able to do this, then they will become completely dependent on the results from data mining, and they won't think for themselves. There is a ton of information that comes from the data mining process, but you must think it through and combine your knowledge and expertise to get the best results.

Of course, this is not to say that the management needs to be data scientists to understand the information and to use it. It just means that the managers of an organization at least need to know some of the basics to appreciate the different opportunities that it will provide. You do not want to waste the valuable resources that data science can provide simply because you don't understand how it works or what all it can do for you and your company.

As a manager, there are a few things that you should be able to do, even if you are not a data scientist. You should be able to appreciate all the opportunities that this information provides, make sure that your data science team has the resources that it needs to get the job done and be willing to invest your time and money so that data experimentation occurs. Finally, you must be able to work with your team to ensure that they stay on track and help you get information to help move the business forward.

How data science gives a competitive advantage

Data science, as long as it is used correctly, can give a business a big competitive edge in their market. To have an advantage over the competition, you must make sure that you are always one to two steps ahead of them. This can be done through a willingness and the act of investing in new data assets and also the development of new capabilities and techniques. It also requires that you not only treat the investment and the results from this as an asset, but you must also treat your data science team and the field of data science in the same way.

With the best data science team, you will be able to gain the useful insights that you need to help move your business into the future. There are so many businesses that will just rely on experience and knowledge to help them. And if you have been in the industry for a long time, you will probably do well. Most of those who are new to an industry will end up failing with this though.

However, even if you are doing well, data science could provide you with some useful information and open up new doors that you may not have thought about in the past.

Chapter 3. history of data science

The history of deep learning can be traced back to 1943, when Warren McCulloch and Walter Pitts published a paper with a concept of Artificial Neuron(AN) to mimic the thought process. This Artificial neuron was based on the characteristic of a biological neuron of either being fully active to a stimulation or none at all. This behavior of biological neurons was observed in microelectrode readings from brain.

In 1957, Frank and Rosenblatt presented Mark I Perceptron Machine as the first implementation of the perceptron algorithm. The idea was to resemble the working of biological neurons to create an agent that can learn. This perceptron was a supervised binary linear classifier with adjustable weights. This functionality was implemented through following function:

Where, w is weights vector, X is inputs and b is bias.

For each input and output pair, this formula provided classification results. If the result/prediction did not match with output, the weight vector was updated through :

Where, is predicted/output of function, is actual output, is input vector and is weight vector.

It should be noted that back at that time, they implemented this functionality through a hardware machine with wires and connections (as shown in the figure below).

In 1960, Widrow and Hoff stacked these perceptrons and built a 3-layered (input layer, hidden layer, output layer), fully connected, feed-forward architecture for classification as a hardware implementation, called ADALINE. The architecture presented in the paper is shown in image below.

In 1960, Henry J. Kelley introduced a continuous back propagation model, which is currently used in learning weights of the model. In 1962, a simpler version of backpropagation based on chain rule was introduced by Stuart Dreyfus but these methods were inefficient. The backpropagation currently used in models was actually presented in 1980s.

In 1979, Fukushima designed a multi-layered convolutional neural network architecture, called Neocognitron, that could learn to recognize patterns in images. The network resembled to current day architectures but wasn't exactly the same. It also allowed to manually adjust the weight of certain connections. Many concepts from Neocognitron continue to be used. The layered connections in perceptrons allowed to develop a variety of neural networks. For several patterns present in the data, Selective Attention Model could distinguish and separate them.

In 1970, Seppo Linnainmaa presented automatic differentiation to efficiently compute the derivative of a differentiable composite function using chain rule. Its application, later in 1986, led to the backpropagation of errors in multilayer perceptrons. This was when Geoff Hinton, Williams and Rumelhart presented a paper to demonstrate that backpropagation in neural networks provides interesting distribution representations. In 1989, Yann LeCun, currently, Director of AI Research Facebook, provided first practical demonstration of backpropagation in convolutional neural networks to read handwritten digits at Bell Labs. Even though with backpropagation, deep neural networks were not being able to train well.

In 1995, Vapnik and Cortes introduced support vector machines for regression and classification of data. In 1997, Schmidhuber and Hochreiter introduced Long Short Term Memory (LSTM) for recurrent neural networks.

In all these years, a major hindering constraint was computed but in 1999, computers started to become faster at processing data and Graphical Processing Units (GPUs) were introduced. This immensely increased the compute power.

In 2006, Hinton and Salakhutdinov presented a paper that reinvigorated research in deep learning. This was the first time when a proper 10 layer convolutional neural network was trained properly. Instead of training 10 layers using backpropagation, they came up with an unsupervised pre-training scheme, called Restricted Boltzmann Machine. This was a 2 step approach for training. In the first step, each layer of the network was trained using unsupervised objective. In the second step, all the layers were stacked together for backpropagation.

Later in 2009, Fei-Fei Li, a professor at Stanford university launched ImageNet, a large visual database designed for visual object recognition research containing more than 14 million hand-annotated images of 20,000 different object categories. This gave neural networks a huge edge as data of this order made it possible to train neural networks and achieve good results.

In 2010, neural networks got a lot of attention from the research community when Microsoft presented a paper on speech recognition and neural networks performed really well compared to other machine learning tools like SVMs and kernels. Specifically, they introduced neural network as a part of GMM and HMM framework and achieved huge improvements.

In 2012, a paper by Krizhevsky, Sutskever and Hinton showed that huge improvements are achieved through deep learning in the visual recognition domain. Their model, AlexNet outperformed all the other traditional computer vision methods in visual recognition task and won several international competitions. Since then, the field has exploded and several network architectures and ideas have been introduced like GANs.

Chapter 4. data science and artificial intelligence

Machine Learning will study an algorithm and let machines recognize patterns, develop models, and generate videos and images via learning. Machine Learning algorithms can be created using different methods such as clustering, decision trees, linear regression, and many more.

What is an Artificial Neural Network?

Artificial Neural Network is propelled by biological models of brain and biological neural networks. In brief, Artificial Neural Network (ANN) refers to a computational representation of the human neural network which alters human intelligence, memory, and reasoning. But why should the human brain system develop effective ML algorithms?

The major principle behind ANN is that neural networks are effective in advanced computations and hierarchical representation of knowledge. Dendrites and axons connect neurons into complex neural networks that can pass and exchange information as well as store intermediary computation results.

Therefore, a computational model of such systems can be effective in learning processes that resemble biological ones.

The perception algorithm created in 1957 was the trial to build a computational model of a biological neural network. However, advanced neural networks that have multiple layers, neurons, and nodes became possible just recently.

ANN is the reason for the recent success in computer vision and image recognition. Natural Language Processing and other applications of machine language seek to extract complex patterns from data. Neural networks are very useful when one wants to study nonlinear hypothesis that has many features. Building a precise hypothesis for a massive feature space may need one to have multiple high order polynomials that would inevitably result in overfitting. This is a situation where a model reveals random noise in data instead of the underlying patterns of relationships. The issue with overfitting involves image recognition problems. Here, each pixel represents a feature.

A Simple Neural Network That Has a Single Neuron

The simplest neural network has a single 'neuron' as shown below.

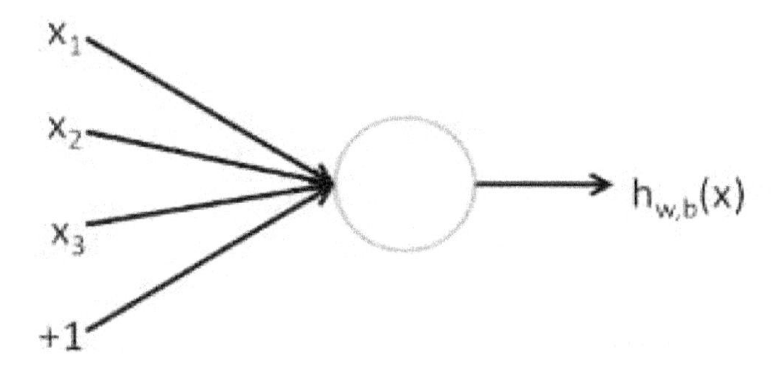

By applying a biological analogy, this neuron represents a computational unit that assumes inputs through electrical inputs and transfers them using axons to the next network output.

In the above simple neural network, dendrites refer to input features (x1, X2) and the output is the result of the hypothesis hw,b(x). Apart from the input features, the input layer of the neural network contains a bias unit that is equivalent to 1. A bias unit is required to apply a constant term in the function hypothesis.

In machine learning, the above network contains a single input layer, a hidden layer, and one output layer. To implement the learning process for this network, the input layer accepts input features for every training sample and feeds it to the activation function which computes the hypothesis in the hidden layer.

An activation function is a logistic regression applied in classification. However, other options are also possible. In the above case, a single neuron is similar to the input-output mapping defined by a logistic regression.

$$y = \varsigma(x) = \frac{1}{1+e^{-x}}$$

Multi-layered Neural Network

To understand how neural network operates, it is important to formalize the model and explain it in a real-world scenario. The image below represents a multilayer network that has three layers and various neurons. In this case, just like a single-neuron network, there is one input layer that has three inputs (x1, x2, x3) that has an added bias unit (+1). The second network layer is a hidden layer that has three units represented by activation functions. This is called a hidden layer because the values that are computed in it aren't observed. Basically, a neural network contains multiple hidden layers that pass advanced computations and functions from surface layers to the bottom of the neural network. The design of a neural network that has a lot of hidden layers is constantly used in Deep Learning.

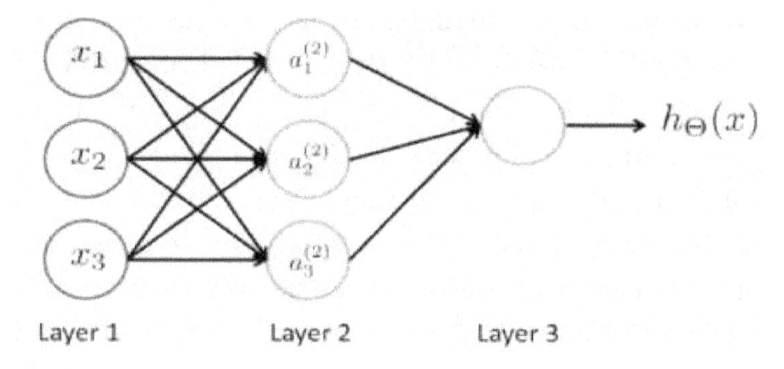

The hidden layer 2 has three neurons (a12, a22, a32). Each neuron of a hidden layer activates layer j. In this case, a unit a1 activates the first neuron of the second layer. Activation means that the value that is computed by function activation in this layer is output by the same node to the next layer.

Layer 3 is the output layer that receives results from the hidden layer and applies its own activation function. This layer calculates the final value of the hypothesis. Next, the cycle continues until that point when the neural network comes up with the model and weights which best predict the values of the training data.

Chapter 5. data science tips and tricks

One of the major strengths of Data Scientists is a strong background in Math and Statistics. Mathematics helps them create complex analytics. Besides this, they also use mathematics to create Machine Learning models and Artificial Intelligence. Similar to software engineering, Data Scientists must interact with the business side. This involves mastering the domain so that they can draw insights. Data Scientists need to analyze data to help a business, and this calls for some business acumen. Lastly, the results need to be assigned to the business in a way that anyone can understand. This calls for the ability to verbally and visually communicate advanced results and observations in a manner that a business can understand as well as work on it.

Therefore, it is important for any wannabe Data Scientists to have knowledge about Data Mining. Data Mining describes the process where raw data is structured in such a way where one can recognize patterns in the data via mathematical and computational algorithms.

Below are five mining techniques that every data scientist should know:

1. **MapReduce**

The modern Data Mining applications need to manage vast amounts of data rapidly. To deal with these applications, one must use a new software stack. Since programming systems can retrieve parallelism from a computing cluster, a software stack has a new file system called a distributed file system.

The system has a larger unit than the disk blocks found in the normal operating system. A distributed file system replicates data to enforce security against media failures.

In addition to such file systems, a higher-level programming system has also been created. This is referred to as MapReduce. It is a form of computing which has been implemented in different systems such as Hadoop and Google's implementation. You can adopt a MapReduce implementation to control large-scale computations such that it can deal with hardware faults. You only need to write three functions. That is **Map** and **Reduce**, and then you can allow the system to control parallel execution and task collaboration.

2. Distance Measures

The major problem with Data Mining is reviewing data for similar items. An example can be searching for a collection of web pages and discovering duplicate pages. Some of these pages could be plagiarism or pages that have almost identical content but different in content. Other examples can include customers who buy similar products or discover images with similar characteristics.

Distance measure basically refers to a technique that handles this problem. It searches for the nearest neighbors in a higher dimensional space. For every application, it is important to define the meaning of similarity. The most popular definition is the Jaccard Similarity. It refers to the ratio between intersection sets and union. It is the best similarity to reveal textual similarity found in documents and certain behaviors of customers.

For example, when looking for identical documents, there are different instances of this particular example. There might be very many small pieces of one document appearing out of order, more documents for comparisons, and documents that are so large to fit in the main memory. To handle these issues, there are three important steps to finding similar documents.

- ***Shingling.*** This involves converting documents into sets.
- ***Min-Hashing.*** It involves converting a large set into short signatures while maintaining similarity.
- ***Locality Sensitive Hashing***. Concentrate on signature pairs that might be from similar documents.

The most powerful way that you can represent documents assets is to retrieve a set of short strings from the document.

- A k-Shingle refers to any k characters that can show up in a document.
- A min-hash functions on sets.
- Locality-Sensitive Hashing.

3. Link Analysis

Traditional search engines did not provide accurate search results because of spam vulnerability. However, Google managed to overcome this problem by using the following technique:

- PageRank. It uses simulation. If a user surfing a web page starts from a random page, PageRank attempts to congregate in case it had monitored specific outlines from the page that users are located. This whole process works iteratively meaning pages that have a higher number of users are ranked better than pages without users visiting.

- The content in a page was determined by the specific phrases used in the page and linked with external pages. Although it is easy for a spammer to modify a page that they are administrators, it is very difficult for them to do the same on an external page which they aren't administrators.

In other words, PageRank represents a function that allocates a real number to a web page. The intention is that a page with a higher page rank becomes more important than a page that does not have a page rank. There is no fixed algorithm defined to assign a page rank, but there are different varieties.

For powerfully connected Web Graphs, PageRank applies the principle of the transition matrix. This principle is useful for calculating the rank of a page.

To calculate the behavior of a page rank, it simulates the actions of random users on a page.

There are different enhancements that one can make to PageRank. The first one is called Topic-Sensitive PageRank. This type of improvement can weigh certain pages more heavily as a result of their topic. If you are aware of the query on a particular page, then it is possible to be based on the rank of the page.

4. **Data Streaming**

In most of the Data Mining situations, you can't know the whole data set in advance. There are times when data arrives in the form of a stream, and then gets processed immediately before it disappears forever.

Furthermore, the speed at which data arrives very fast, and that makes it hard to store in the active storage. In short, the data is infinite and non-stationary. Stream management, therefore, becomes very important.

In the data stream management system, there is no limit to the number of streams that can fit into a system. Each data stream produces elements at its own time. The elements should then have the same data rates and time in a particular stream.

Streams can be archived into a store, but this will make it impossible to reply to queries from the archival store. This can later be analyzed under special cases by using a specific retrieval method.

Furthermore, there is a working store where summaries are placed so that one can use to reply to queries. The active store can either be a disk or main memory. It all depends on the speed at which one wants to process the queries. Whichever way, it does not have the right capacity to store data from other streams.

Data streaming has different problems as highlighted below:

- Sampling Data in a Stream

To create a sample of the stream that is used in a class of queries, you must select a set of attributes to be used in a stream. By hashing the key of an incoming stream element, the hash value can be the best to help determine whether all or none of the elements in the key belong to the sample.

- Filtering Streams

To accept tuples that fit a specific criterion, accepted tuples should go through a separate process of the stream while the rest of the tuples are eliminated. Bloom filtering is a wonderful technique that one can use to filter streams to allow elements in a given set to pass through while foreign elements are deleted.

Members in the selected set are hashed into buckets to form bits. The bits are then set to 1. If you would like to test an element of a stream, you must hash the element into a set of bits using the hash function.

- Count Specific Elements in a Stream

Consider stream elements chosen from a universal set. If you wanted to know the number of unique elements that exist in a stream, you might have to count from the start of the stream. Flajolet-Martin is a method which often hashes elements to integers, described as binary numbers. By using a lot of the hash functions and integrating these estimates, you finally get a reliable estimate.

5. Frequent Item – Set Analysis

The market-basket model features many relationships. On one side, there are items, and on the opposite side, there are baskets. Every basket contains a set of items. The hypothesis created here is that the number of items in the basket is always smaller than the total number of items. This means that if you count the items in the basket, it should be high and large to fit in memory. Here, data is similar to a file that has a series of baskets. In reference to the distributed file system, baskets represent the original file. Each basket is of type "set of items".

As a result, a popular family technique to characterize data depending on the market-basket model is to discover frequent item-sets. These are sets of items that reveal the most baskets.

Market basket analysis was previously applied in supermarket and chain stores. These stores track down the contents of each market basket that a customer brings to the checkout. Items represent products sold by the store while baskets are a set of items found in a single basket.

That said, this same model can be applied in many different data types such as:

• **Similar concepts.** Let items represent words and baskets documents. Therefore, a document or basket has words or items available in the document. If you were to search for words that are repeated in a document, sets would contain the most words.

• **Plagiarism.** You can let the items represent documents and baskets to be sentenced.

Properties of Frequent-Item Sets to Know

- **Association rules**. These refer to implications in case a basket has a specific set of items.

- **Monotonicity**. One of the most important properties of item-sets is that if a set is frequent, then all its subsets are frequent.

Part 2: DATA SCIENCE WITH PYTHON

Chapter 6. Introduction to NumPy

Now that you know the basics of loading and preprocessing data with the help of pandas, we can move on to data processing with NumPy. The purpose of this stage is to have a data matrix ready for the next stage, which involves supervised and unsupervised machine learning mechanisms. NumPy data structure comes in the form of ndarray objects, and this is what you will later feed into the machine learning process. For now, we will start by creating such an object to better understand this phase.

The n-dimensional Array

As we discussed in the chapter about Python fundamental data types, lists and dictionaries are some of Python's most important structures. You can build complex data structures with them because they are powerful at storing data, however they're not great at operating on that data. They aren't optimal when it comes to processing power and speed, which are critical when working with complex algorithms. This is why we're using NumPy and its ndarray object, which stands for an "n-dimensional array". Let's look at the properties of a NumPy array:

1. **It is optimal and fast at transferring data. When you work with complex data, you want the memory to handle it efficiently instead of being bottlenecked.**
2. **You can perform vectorization. In other words, you can make linear algebra computations and specific element operations without being forced to use "for" loops. This is a large plus for NumPy because Python "for" loops cost a lot of resources, making it really expensive to work with a large number of loops instead of ndarrays.**

3. **In data science operations you will have to use tools, or libraries, such as SciPy and Scikit-learn. You can't use them without arrays because they are required as an input, otherwise functions won't perform as intended.**

With that being said, here are a few methods of creating a ndarray:

1. **Take an already existing data structure and turn into an array.**
2. **Build the array from the start and add in the values later.**
3. **You can also upload data to an array even when it's stored on a disk.**

Converting a list to a one-dimensional array is a fairly common operation in data science processes. Keep in mind that you have to take into account the type of objects such a list contains. This will have an impact on the dimensionality of the result. Here's an example of this with a list that contains only integers:

```
In: import numpy as np

int_list = [1,2,3]

Array_1 = np.array(int_list)

In: Array_1

Out: array([1, 2, 3])
```

You can access the array just like you access a list in Python. You simply use indexing, and just like in Python, it starts from 0. This is how this operation would look:

In: Array_1[1]

Out: 2

Now you can gain more data about the objects inside the array like so:

In: type(Array_1)

Out: numpy.ndarray

In: Array_1.dtype

Out: dtype('int64')

The result of the dtype is related to the type of operating system you're running. In this example, we're using a 64 bit operating system.

At the end of this exercise, our basic list is transformed into a uni-dimensional array. But what happens if we have a list that contains more than just one type of element? Let's say we have integers, strings, and floats. Let's see an example of this:

In: import numpy as np

composite_list = [1,2,3] + [1.,2.,3.] + ['a','b','c']

Array_2 = np.array(composite_list[:3])#here we have only integers

print ('composite_list[:3]', Array_2.dtype)

Array_2 = np.array(composite _list[:6]) #now we have integers and floats

print (' composite _list[:6]', Array_2.dtype)

```
Array_2 = np.array(composite _list) #strings have been added to the array

print (' composite _list[:] ',Array_2.dtype)
```

Out:

```
composite _list[:3] int64

composite _list[:6] float64

composite _list[:] <U32
```

As you can see, we have a "composite_list" that contains integers, floats, and strings. It's important to understand that when we make an array, we can have any kind of data types and mix them however we wish.

Next, let's see how we can load an array from a file. N-dimensional arrays can be created from the data contained inside a file. Here's an example in code:

```
In: import numpy as np

cars = np.loadtxt('regression-datasets

cars.csv',delimiter=',', dtype=float)
```

In this example, we tell our tool to create an array from a file with the help of the "loadtxt" method by giving it a filename, delimiter, and a data type.

Chapter 7. packages installations

To get started with NumPy, we have to install the package into our version of Python. While the basic method for installing packages to Python is the ***pip install*** method, we will be using the ***conda install*** method. This is the recommended way of managing all Python packages and virtual environments using the anaconda framework.

Since we installed a recent version of Anaconda, most of the packages we need would have been included in the distribution. To verify if any package is installed, you can use the ***conda list*** command via the anaconda prompt. This displays all the packages currently installed and accessible via anaconda. If your intended package is not available, then you can install via this method:

First, ensure you have an internet connection. This is required to download the target package via conda. Open the anaconda prompt, then enter the following code:

Conda install **package**

***Note**: In the code above, 'package' is what needs to be installed e.g. NumPy, Pandas, etc.*

As described earlier, we would be working with NumPy arrays. In programming, an array is an ordered collection of similar items. Sounds familiar? Yeah, they are just like Python lists, but with superpowers. NumPy arrays are in two forms: Vectors, and Matrices. They are mostly the same, only that vectors are one-dimensional arrays (either a column or a row of ordered items), while a matrix is 2-dimensional (rows and columns). These are the fundamental blocks of most operations we would be doing with NumPy. While arrays incorporate most of the operations possible with Python lists, we would be introducing some newer methods for creating, and manipulating them.

To begin using the NumPy methods, we have to first import the package into our current workspace. This can be achieved in two ways:

```
import numpy as np

Or

from numpy import *
```

In Jupyter notebook, enter either of the codes above to import the NumPy package. The first method of import is recommended, especially for beginners, as it helps to keep track of the specific package a called function/method is from. This is due to the variable assignment e.g. ‘np’, which refers to the imported package throughout the coding session.

Notice the use of an asterisk in the second import method. This signifies ‘everything/all’ in programming. Hence, the code reads **‘from NumPy import everything!!’**

Tip: *In Python, we would be required to reference the package we are operating with e.g. NumPy, Pandas, etc. It is easier to assign them variable names that can be used in further operations. This is significantly useful in a case where there are multiple packages being used, and the use of standard variable names such as: ‘np’ for NumPy, ‘pd’ for Pandas, etc. makes the code more readable.*

Example: Creating vectors and matrices from Python lists.

Let us declare a Python list.

```
In []: # This is a list of integers
 Int_list = [1,2,3,4,5]
     Int_list

Out[]: [1,2,3,4,5]
```

Importing the NumPy package and creating an array of integers.

```
In []: # import syntax
import numpy as np
np.array(Int_list)

Out[]: array([1, 2, 3, 4, 5])
```

Notice the difference in the outputs? The second output indicates that we have created an array, and we can easily assign this array to a variable for future reference.

To confirm, we can check for the type.

```
In []: x = np.array(Int_list)

       type(x)

Out[]: numpy.ndarray
```

We have created a vector, because it has one dimension (1 row). To check this, the 'ndim' method can be used.

```
In []: x.ndim   # this shows how many dimensions the array has
Out[]: 1
```

Alternatively, the shape method can be used to see the arrangements.

```
In []: x.shape  # this shows the shape

Out[]: (5,)
```

Python describes matrices as ***(rows, columns)***. In this case, it describes a vector as ***(number of elements,)***. To create a matrix from a Python list, we need to pass a nested list containing the elements we need. Remember, matrices are rectangular, and so each list in the nested list must have the same size.

```
In []: # This is a matrix


 x = [1,2,3]
 y = [4,5,6]


 my_list = [y,x]  # nested list


 my_matrix = np.array(my_list)  # creating the matrix


 A = my_matrix.ndim
 B = my_matrix.shape


 # Printing
 print('Resulting matrix:\n\n',my_matrix,'\n\nDimensions:',A,
 '\nshape (rows,columns):',B)


Out[]: Resulting matrix:


[[4 5 6]
[1 2 3]]
```

Dimensions: 2

shape (rows,columns): (2, 3)

Now, we have created a 2 by 3 matrix. Notice how the shape method displays the rows and columns of the matrix. To find the transpose of this matrix i.e. change the rows to columns, use the ***transpose ()*** method.

```
In []: # this finds the transpose of the matrix

t_matrix = my_matrix.transpose()

    t_matrix

Out[]: array([[4, 1],

    [5, 2],

    [6, 3]])
```

Tip: *Another way of knowing the number of dimensions of an array is by counting the square-brackets that opens and closes the array (immediately after the parenthesis). In the vector example, notice that the array was enclosed in single square brackets. In the two-dimensional array example, however, there are two brackets. Also, tuples can be used in place of lists for creating arrays.*

There are other methods of creating arrays in Python, and they may be more intuitive than using lists in some applications. One quick method uses the ***arange()*** function.

Syntax: np.arange(start value, stop value, step size, dtype = 'type')
In this case, we do not need to pass its output to the list function, our result is an array object of a data type specified by 'dtype'.

Example: Creating arrays with the arange() function.

We will create an array of numbers from 0 to 10, with an increment of 2 (even numbers).

```
In []: # Array of even numbers between 0 and 10

Even_array = np.arange(0,11,2)

Even_array
```

```
Out[]: array([ 0,  2,  4,  6,  8, 10])
```

Notice it behaves like the range () method form our list examples. It returned all even values between 0 and 11 (10 being the maximum). Here, we did not specify the types of the elements.

Tip: *Recall, the range method returns value up to the 'stop value – 1'; hence, even if we change the 11 to 12, we would still get 10 as the maximum.*

Since the elements are numeric, they can either be integers or floats. Integers are the default, however, to return the values as floats, we can also specify the numeric type.

In []: Even_array2 = np.arange(0,11,2, dtype='float')

Even_array2

Out[]: array([0., 2., 4., 6., 8., 10.])

Another handy function for creating arrays is ***linspace()***. This returns a numeric array of linearly space values within an interval. It also allows for the specification of the required number of points, and it has the following syntax:

np.linspace(start value, end value, number of points)

At default, linspace returns an array of 50 evenly spaced points within the defined interval.

Example: Creating arrays of evenly spaced points with linspace()

```
In []: # Arrays of linearly spaced points
A = np.linspace(0,5,5) # 5 equal points between 0 & 5
B = np.linspace (51,100) # 50 equal points between 51 & 100
    print ('Here are the arrays:\n')
A
B

Here are the arrays:
```

```
Out[ ]: array([0.  , 1.25, 2.5 , 3.75, 5.  ])

Out[ ]: array([ 1.,  2.,  3.,  4.,  5.,  6.,  7.,  8.,  9., 10., 11., 12., 13.,
        14., 15., 16., 17., 18., 19., 20., 21., 22., 23., 24., 25., 26.,
        27., 28., 29., 30., 31., 32., 33., 34., 35., 36., 37., 38., 39.,
        40., 41., 42., 43., 44., 45., 46., 47., 48., 49., 50.])
```

Notice how the second use of linspace did not require a third argument. This is because we wanted 50 equally spaced values, which is the default. The 'dtype' can also be specified like we did with the range function.

Tip 1: *Linspace arrays are particularly useful in plots. They can be used to create a time axis or any other required axis for producing well defined and scaled graphs.*

Tip 2: *The output format in the example above is not the default way for output in Jupyter notebook. Jupyter displays the last result per cell, at default. To display multiple results (without having to use the print statement every-time), the output method can be*

changed using the following code.

```
In[]: # Allowing Jupyter output all results per cell.
# run the following code in a Jupyter cell.

 from IPython.core.interactiveshell import InteractiveShell
 InteractiveShell.ast_node_interactivity = "all"
```

There are times when a programmer needs unique arrays like the identity matrix, or a matrix of ones/zeros. NumPy provides a convenient way of creating these with the ***zeros()***, ***ones()*** and ***eye()*** functions.

Example: creating arrays with unique elements.

Let us use the zeros () function to create a vector and a matrix.

```
In []: np.zeros(3)  # A vector of 3 elements
 np.zeros((2,3)) # A matrix of 6 elements i.e. 2 rows, 3 columns
```

Out[]: array([0., 0., 0.])

Out[]: array([[0., 0., 0.],

[0., 0., 0.]])

Notice how the second output is a two-dimensional array i.e. two square brackets (a matrix of 2 columns and 3 rows as specified in the code).

The same thing goes for creating a vector or matrix with all elements having a value of '1'.

```
In []: np.ones(3)  # A vector of 3 elements
 np.ones((2,3)) # A matrix of 6 elements i.e. 2 rows, 3 columns
```

```
Out[]: array([1., 1., 1.])

Out[]: array([[1., 1., 1.],

       [1., 1., 1.]])
```

Also, notice how the code for creating the matrices requires the row and column instructions to be passed as a tuple. This is because the function accepts one input, so multiple inputs would need to be passed as tuples or lists in the required order (Tuples are recommended. Recall, they are faster to operate.).

In the case of the identity matrix, the function eye () only requires one value. Since identity matrices are always square, the value passed determines the number of rows and columns.

```
In []: np.eye(2) # A matrix of 4 elements 2 rows, 2 columns
 np.eye(3) # 3 rows, 3 columns

Out[]: array([[1., 0.],
        [0., 1.]])
Out[]: array([[1., 0., 0.],
        [0., 1., 0.],
        [0., 0., 1.]])
```

NumPy also features random number generators. These can be used for creating arrays, as well as single values, depending on the required application. To access the random number generator, we call the library via ***np.random***, and then choose the random method we prefer. We will consider three methods for generating random numbers: ***rand()***, ***randn()***, and ***randint()***.

Example: Generating arrays with random values.

Let us start with the rand () method. This generates random, uniformly distributed numbers between 0 and 1.

```
In []: np.random.rand (2)   # A vector of 2 random values
 np.random.rand (2,3)  # A matrix of 6 random values

Out[]: array([0.01562571, 0.54649508])
Out[]: array([[0.22445055, 0.35909056, 0.53403529],
        [0.70449515, 0.96560456, 0.79583743]])
```

Notice how each value within the arrays are between 0 & 1. You can try this on your own and observe the returned values. Since it is a random generation, these values may be different from yours. Also, in the case of the random number generators, the matrix specifications are not required to be passed as lists or tuples, as observed in the second line of code.

The randn () method generates random numbers from the standard normal or Gaussian distribution. You might want to brush up on some basics in statistics, however, this just implies that the values returned would have a tendency towards the mean (which is zero in this case) i.e. the values would be centered around zero.

```
In []: np.random.randn (2)   # A vector of 2 random values
 np.random.randn (2,3)  # A matrix of 6 random values

Out[]: array([ 0.73197866, -0.31538023])
```

```
Out[]: array([[-0.79848228, -0.7176693 , 0.74770505],
       [-2.10234448,  0.10995745, -0.54636425]])
```

The randint() method generates random integers within a specified range or interval. Note that the higher range value is exclusive (i.e. has no chance of being randomly selected), while the lower value is inclusive (could be included in the random selection).

Syntax: `np.random(lower value, higher value, number of values, dtype)`
If the number of values is not specified, Python just returns a single value within the defined range.

```
In []: np.random.randint (1,5)        # A random value between 1
          and 5
 np.random.randint (1,100,6)   # A vector of 6 random values
np.random.randint (1,100,(2,3)) # A matrix of 6 random values
Out[]: 4
Out[]: array([74, 42, 92, 10, 76, 43])
Out[]: array([[92,  9, 99],
        [73, 36, 93]])
```

Tip: *Notice how the size parameter for the third line was specified using a tuple. This is how to create a matrix of random integers using randint.*

Example: Illustrating randint().

Let us create a fun dice roll program using the randint() method. We would allow two dice, and the function will return an output based on the random values generated in the roll.

```
In []: # creating a dice roll game with randint()
 # Defining the function
 def roll_dice():
       """ This function displays a
       dice roll value when called"""

     dice1  =  np.random.randint(1,7)  # This allows 6 to be
                      inclusive

       dice2 = np.random.randint(1,7)

# Display Condition.
       if dice1 == dice2:
     print('Roll: ',dice1,'&',dice2,'\ndoubles !')
         if dice1 == 1:
             print('snake eyes!\n')
       else:
      print('Roll: ',dice1,'&',dice2)
```

```
In []: # Calling the function
 roll_dice()

Out[]: Roll:  1 & 1
 doubles !
 snake eyes!
```

Hint: *Think of a fun and useful program to illustrate the use of these random number generators, and writing such programs will improve your chances of comprehension. Also, a quick review of statistics, especially measures of central tendency & dispersion/spread will be useful in your data science journey.*

Chapter 8. manipulating array

Now that we have learned how to declare arrays, we would be proceeding with some methods for modifying these arrays. First, we will consider the ***reshape ()*** method, which is used for changing the dimensions of an array.

Example: Using the reshape() method.

Let us declare a few arrays and call the reshape method to change their dimensions.

```
In []: freq = np.arange(10);values = np.random.randn(10)
    freq; values

Out[]: array([0, 1, 2, 3, 4, 5, 6, 7, 8, 9])
```

Out[]: array([1.33534821, 1.73863505, 0.1982571 , -0.47513784, 1.80118596, -1.73710743, -0.24994721, 1.41695744, -0.28384007, 0.58446065])

Using the reshape method, we would make 'freq' and 'values' 2 dimensional.

```
In []: np.reshape(freq,(5,2))

Out[]: array([[0, 1],
    [2, 3],
    [4, 5],
    [6, 7],
    [8, 9]])
```

```
In []: np.reshape(values,(2,5))

Out[]: array([[ 1.33534821,  1.73863505,  0.1982571 , -
        0.47513784, 1.80118596],
 [-1.73710743,  -0.24994721,  1.41695744,  -
        0.28384007, 0.58446065]])
```

Even though the values array still looks similar after reshaping, notice the two square brackets that indicate it has been changed to a matrix. The reshape method comes in handy when we need to do array operations, and our arrays are inconsistent in dimensions. It is also important to ensure the new size parameter passed to the reshape method does not differ from the number of elements in the original array. The idea is simple: when calling the reshape method, the product of the size parameters must equal the number of elements in the original array.

The maximum and minimum values within an array (or real-world data), and possibly the index of such maximum or minimum values. To get this information, we can use the ***.max()***, ***.min()***, ***.argmax()*** and ***.argmin()*** methods respectively.

Example:
Let us find the maximum and minimum values in the 'values' array, along with the index of the minimum and maximum within the array.

```
In []: A = values.max();B = values.min();
    C = values.argmax()+1; D = values.argmin()+1

    print('Maximum value: {}\nMinimum Value: {}\
```

```
    \nItem {} is the maximum value, while item {}\
is the minimum value'.format(A,B,C,D))
```

Output

```
Maximum value: 1.8011859577930067
Minimum Value: -1.7371074259180737

Item 5 is the maximum value, while item 6 is the minimum value
```

A few things to note in the code above: The variables C&D, which defines the position of the maximum and minimum values are evaluated as shown [by adding 1 to the index of the maximum and minimum values obtained via ***argmax ()*** and ***argmin ()***], because Python indexing starts at zero. Python would index maximum value at 4, and minimum at 5, which is not the actual positions of these elements within the array (you are less likely to start counting elements in a list from zero! Unless you are Python, of course.).

Another observation can be made in the code. The print statement is broken across a few lines using enter. To allow Python to know that the next line of code is a continuation, the backslash '\' is used. Another way would be to use three quotes for a multiline string.

Chapter 9. conditional selection,

Similar to how we conditional selection works with NumPy arrays, we can select elements from a data frame that satisfy a Boolean criterion.

Example: Let us grab sections of the data frame 'Arr_df' where the value is > 5.

In []: # Grab elements greater than five

Arr_df[Arr_df>5]

Output:

	odd1	even1	odd2	even2	Odd sum	Even sum
A	NaN	NaN	NaN	NaN	NaN	6
B	NaN	6.0	7.0	8.0	12.0	14
C	9.0	10.0	11.0	12.0	20.0	22
D	13.0	14.0	15.0	16.0	28.0	30
E	17.0	18.0	19.0	20.0	36.0	38

Notice how the instances of values less than 5 are represented with a 'NaN'.

Another way to use this conditional formatting is to format based on column specifications.

You could remove entire rows of data, by specifying a Boolean condition based off a single column. Assuming we want to return the Arr_df data frame without the row 'C'. We can specify a condition to return values where the elements of column 'odd1' are not equal to '9' (since row C contains 9 under column 'odd1').

In []: # removing row C through the first column

```
Arr_df[Arr_df['odd1']!= 9]
```

Output:

	odd1	even1	odd2	even2	Odd sum	Even sum
A	1	2	3	4	4	6
B	5	6	7	8	12	14
D	13	14	15	16	28	30
E	17	18	19	20	36	38

Notice that row 'C' has been filtered out. This can be achieved through a smart conditional statement through any of the columns.

In []: # does the same thing : remove row 'C'

```
# Arr_df[Arr_df['even2']!= 12]
```

In[]: # Let us remove rows D and E through 'even2'

```
Arr_df[Arr_df['even2']<= 12]
```

Output

	odd1	even1	odd2	even2	Odd sum	Even sum
A	1	2	3	4	4	6
B	5	6	7	8	12	14
C	9	10	11	12	20	22

Exercise: Remove rows C, D, E via the ‘Even sum’ column. Also, try out other such operations as you may prefer.

To combine conditional selection statements, we can use the ‘logical and, i.e. &’, and the ‘logical or, i.e. |’ for nesting multiple conditions. The regular ‘and’ and ‘or’ operators would not work in this case as they are used for comparing single elements. Here, we will be comparing a series of elements that evaluate to true or false, and those generic operators find such operations ambiguous.

Example: Let us select elements that meet the criteria of being greater than 1 in the first column, and less than 22 in the last column. Remember, the ‘and statement’ only evaluates to true if both conditions are true.

In []:Arr_df[(Arr_df['odd1']>1) & (Arr_df['Even sum']<22)]

Output:

	odd1	even1	odd2	even2	Odd sum	Even sum
B	**5**	**6**	**7**	**8**	**12**	**14**

Only the elements in Row ‘B’ meet this criterion, and were returned in the data frame.

This approach can be expounded upon to create even more powerful data frame filters.

Chapter 10. NumPy Array Operations,

Sometimes, when you work with two dimensional arrays, you may want to add new rows or columns to represent new data and variables. This operation is known as array stacking, and it doesn't take long for NumPy to render the new information. Start by creating a new array:

```
In: import numpy as np

dataset = np.arange(50).reshape(10,5)
```

Next, add a new row, and several lines that will be concatenated:

```
In: single_line = np.arange(1*5).reshape(1,5)

several_lines = np.arange(3*5).reshape(3,5)
```

Now let's use the vstack method, which stands for vertical stack, to add a new single line.

```
In: np.vstack((dataset,single_line))
```

This command line will also work if we want to add several lines.

```
In: np.vstack((dataset,several_lines))
```

Next, let's see how to add a variable to the array. This is done with the "hstack" method, which stands for horizontal stack. Here's an example:

```
In: bias = np.ones(10).reshape(10,1) np.hstack((dataset,bias))
```

In this line of code, we added a bias of unit values to the array we created earlier.

As an aspiring data scientist, you will only need to know how to add new rows and columns to your arrays. In most projects you won't need to do more than that, so practice working with two dimensional arrays and NumPy, because this tool is engraved in data science.

Chapter 11. Pandas,

Pandas is built on NumPy and they are meant to be used together. This makes it extremely easy to extract arrays from the data frames. Once these arrays are extracted, they can be turned into data frames themselves. Let's take a look at an example:

```
In: import pandas as pd

import numpy as np

marketing_filename = 'regression-datasets-marketing.csv'

marketing = pd.read_csv(marketing _filename, header=None)
```

In this phase we are uploading data to a data frame. Next, we're going to use the "values" method in order to extract an array that is of the same type as those contained inside the data frame.

```
In: marketing _array = marketing.values

marketing _array.dtype

Out: dtype('float64')
```

We can see that we have a float type array. You can anticipate the type of the array by first using the "dtype" method. This will establish which types are being used by the specified data frame object. Do this before extracting the array. This is how this operation would look:

```
In: marketing.dtypes

Out:  0float64

1 int64
```

2float64

3 int64

4float64

5float64

6float64

7float64

8int64

9int64

10int64

11float64

12float64

13float64

dtype: object

Matrix Operations

This includes matrix calculations, such as matrix to matrix multiplication. Let's create a two dimensional array.

This is a two dimensional array of numbers from 0 to 24. Next, we will declare a vector of coefficients and a column that will stack the vector and its reverse. Here's what it would look like:

In: coefs = np.array([1., 0.5, 0.5, 0.5, 0.5])

coefs_matrix = np.column_stack((coefs,coefs[::-1]))

print (coefs_matrix)

Out:

[[1. 0.5]

[0.50.5]

[0.50.5]

[0.50.5]

[0.51.]]

Now we can perform the multiplication. Here's an example of multiplying the array with the vector:

In: np.dot(M,coefs)

Out: array([5.,20.,35.,50.,65.])

Here's an example of multiplication between the array and the coefficient vectors:

In: np.dot(M,coefs_matrix)

Out:array([[5.,7.],

[20.,22.],

[35.,37.],

[50.,52.],

[65.,67.]])

In both of these multiplication operations, we used the "np.dot" function in order to achieve them. Next up, let's discuss slicing and indexing.

Slicing and Indexing

Indexing is great for viewing the ndarray by sending an instruction to visualize the slice of columns and rows or the index.

Let's start by creating a 10x10 array. It will initially be two-dimensional.

In: import numpy as np

M = np.arange(100, dtype=int).reshape(10,10)

Next let's extract the rows from 2 to 8, but only the ones that are evenly numbered.

In: M[2:9:2,:]

Out:array([[20, 21, 22, 23, 24, 25, 26, 27, 28, 29],

[40, 41, 42, 43, 44, 45, 46, 47, 48, 49],

[60, 61, 62, 63, 64, 65, 66, 67, 68, 69],

[80, 81, 82, 83, 84, 85, 86, 87, 88, 89]])

Now let's extract the column, but only the ones from index 5.

In: M[2:9:2,5:]

Out:array([[25, 26, 27, 28, 29],

[45, 46, 47, 48, 49],

[65, 66, 67, 68, 69],

[85, 86, 87, 88, 89]])

We successfully sliced the rows and the columns. But what happens if we try a negative index? Doing so would reverse the array. Here's how our previous array would look when using a negative index.

In: M[2:9:2,5::-1]

Out:array([[25, 24, 23, 22, 21, 20],

[45, 44, 43, 42, 41, 40],

[65, 64, 63, 62, 61, 60],

[85, 84, 83, 82, 81, 80]])

There are other ways of slicing and indexing the arrays, but for the purposes of this book it's enough to know how to perform the previously mentioned steps. However, keep in mind that this process is only a way of viewing the data. If you want to use these views further by creating new data, you cannot make any modifications in the original arrays. If you do, it can lead to some negative side effects. In that case, you want to use the "copy" method. This will create a copy of the array which you can modify however you wish. Here's the code line for the copy method:

In: N = M[2:9:2,5:].copy()

Chapter 12. Data frames,

A Pandas data frame is just an ordered collection of Pandas series with a common/shared index. At its basic form, a data frame looks more like an excel sheet with rows, columns, labels and headers. To create a data frame, the following syntax is used:

```
pd.DataFrame(data=None, index=None, columns=None,
        dtype=None, copy=False)
```

Usually, the data input is an array of values (of whatever datatype). The index and column parameters are usually lists/vectors of either numeric or string type.

If a Pandas series is passed to a data frame object, the index automatically becomes the columns, and the data points are assigned accordingly.

Example: Creating a data frame

```
In []: df = pd.DataFrame([pool1])      # passing a series

 df                   # show



 # two series

 index = 'WWI WWII'.split()

 new_df = pd.DataFrame([pool1,pool3],index)

 new_df                # show
```

Output:

USA	Britain	France	Germany	
0	1	2	3	4

	USA	Britain	France	Germany
WWI	1	2	3	4
WWII	5	1	3	4

We have created two data frames from the pool 1 and pool 3 series we created earlier. Notice how the first data frame assigns the series labels as column headers, and since no index was assigned, a value of '0' was set at that index i.e. row header.

For the second data frame, the row labels were specified by passing a list of strings ['WWI','WWII'].

Tip: *The* **.split()** *string method is a quick way of creating lists of strings. It works by splitting a string into its component characters, depending on the delimiter passed to the string method.*

For example, let us split this email 'pythonguy@gmail.com' into a

list containing the username and the domain name.

```
In []: # Illustrating the split() method

 email = 'pythonguy@gmail.com'
 string_vec = email.split('@')
 string_vec    # show
```

```
A = string_vec[0]; B = string_vec[1] # Extracting values
print('Username:',A,'\nDomain name:',B)

Out[]: ['pythonguy', 'gmail.com']
   Username: pythonguy

   Domain name: gmail.com
```

To create a data frame with an array, we can use the following method:

```
# Creating dataframe with an array

Array = np.arange(1,21).reshape(5,4)  # numpy array
row_labels = 'A B C D E'.split()
col_labels = 'odd1 even1 odd2 even2'.split()
Arr_df = pd.DataFrame(Array,row_labels,col_labels)
Arr_df
```

Output:

	odd1	even1	odd2	even2
A	1	2	3	4
B	5	6	7	8
C	9	10	11	12
D	13	14	15	16
E	17	18	19	20

Notice how this is not unlike how we create spreadsheets in excel. Try playing around with creating data frames.

Exercise: Create a data frame from a 5 × 4 array of uniformly distributed random values. Include your choice row and column names using the ***.split()*** method.

Hint: *use the rand function to generate your values, and use the reshape method to form an array.*

Now that we can conveniently create Data frames, we are going to learn how to index and grab elements off them.

Tip: *Things to note about data frames.*

- *They are a collection of series (more like a list with Pandas series as its elements).*
- *They are similar to numpy arrays i.e. they are more like n × m dimensional matrices, where 'n' are the rows and 'm' are the columns.*

Example: Grabbing elements from a data frame.

The easiest elements to grab are the columns. This is because, by default, each column element is a series with the row headers as labels. We can grab them by using a similar method from the series – indexing by name.

```
In []: # Grab data frame elements

 Arr_df['odd1']    # grabbing first column

Out[]: A    1
 B    5
```

```
C  9
D  13
E  17
Name: odd1, dtype: int32
```

Pretty easy, right? Notice how the output is like a Pandas series. You can verify this by using the ***type(Arr_df['odd1'])*** command.

When more than one column is grabbed, however, it returns a data frame (which makes sense, since a data frame is a collection of at least two series). To grab more than one column, pass the column names to the indexing as a list. This is shown in the example code below:

```
In []:# Grab two columns

 Arr_df[['odd1','even2']] # grabbing first and last columns
```

Output:

	odd1	even2
A	**1**	**4**
B	**5**	**8**
C	**9**	**12**
D	**13**	**16**
E	**17**	**20**

To select a specific element, use the double square brackets indexing notation we learned under array indexing. For example, let us select the value 15 from Arr_df.

In []: Arr_df['odd2']['D']

Out[]: 15

You may decide to break the steps into two, if it makes it easier. This method is however preferred as it saves memory from variable allocation. To explain, let us break it down into two steps.

```
In []: x = Arr_df['odd2']
x

Out[]: A   3
B   7
C   11
D   15
E   19
Name: odd2, dtype: int32
```

See that the first operation returns a series containing the element ‘15’. This series can now be indexed to grab 15 using the label ‘D’.

In []: x['D']

Out[]: 15

While this approach works, and is preferred by beginners, a better approach is to get comfortable with the first method to save coding time and resources.

To grab rows, a different indexing method is used. You can use either ***data_frame_name.loc['row_name']*** or ***data_frame_name.iloc['row_index']***.

Let us grab the row E from ***Arr_df***.

```
In []: print("using .loc['E']")

    Arr_df.loc['E']



    print('\nusing .iloc[4]')

    Arr_df.iloc[4]



     using .loc['E']

Out[]:

    odd1    17
```

even1 18

odd2 19

even2 20

Name: E, dtype: int32

using .iloc[4]

Out[]:

odd1 17

even1 18

odd2 19

even2 20

Name: E, dtype: int32

See, the same result!

You can also use the row indexing method to select single items.

In []: Arr_df.loc['E']['even2']

 # or

Arr_df.iloc[4]['even2']

Out[]: 20

Out[]: 20

Moving on, we will try to create new columns in a data frame, and also delete a column.

```
In []: # Let us add two sum columns to Arr_df

 Arr_df['Odd sum'] = Arr_df['odd1']+Arr_df['odd2']
 Arr_df['Even sum'] = Arr_df['even1']+Arr_df['even2']

 Arr_df
```

Output:

	odd1	even1	odd2	even2	Odd sum	Even sum
A	1	2	3	4	4	6
B	5	6	7	8	12	14
C	9	10	11	12	20	22
D	13	14	15	16	28	30

E	17	18	19	20	36	38

Notice how the new columns are declared. Also, arithmetic operations are possible with each element in the data frame, just like we did with the series.

Exercise: Add an extra column to this data frame. Call it Total Sum, and it should be the addition of Odd sum and Even sum.

To remove a column from a data frame, we use the ***data_frame_name.drop()*** method.

Let us remove the insert a new column and then remove it using the ***.drop()*** method.

```
In []:
Arr_df['disposable'] = np.zeros(5)  # new column

Arr_df  #show
```

Output:

	odd1	even1	odd2	even2	Odd sum	Even sum	disposable
A	1	2	3	4	4	6	0.0
B	5	6	7	8	12	14	0.0

C	**9**	**10**	**11**	**12**	**20**	**22**	**0.0**
D	**13**	**14**	**15**	**16**	**28**	**30**	**0.0**
E	**17**	**18**	**19**	**20**	**36**	**38**	**0.0**

To remove the unwanted column:

```
In []: # to remove
 Arr_df.drop('disposable',axis=1,inplace=True)
 Arr_df
```

Output:

	odd1	even1	odd2	even2	Odd sum	Even sum
A	**1**	**2**	**3**	**4**	**4**	**6**
B	**5**	**6**	**7**	**8**	**12**	**14**
C	**9**	**10**	**11**	**12**	**20**	**22**
D	**13**	**14**	**15**	**16**	**28**	**30**
E	**17**	**18**	**19**	**20**	**36**	**38**

Notice the ‘axis=1’ and ‘inplace = True’ arguments. These are parameters that specify the location to perform the drop i.e. axis (axis = 0 specifies row operation), and intention to broadcast the drop to the original data frame, respectively. If ‘inplace= False’, the data frame will still contain the dropped column.

Chapter 13. Missing Data,

There are instances when the data being imported or generated into pandas is incomplete or have missing data points. In such a case, the likely solution is to remove such values from the dataset, or to fill in new values based on some statistical extrapolation techniques. While we would not be fully exploring statistical measures of extrapolation (you can read up on that from any good statistics textbook), we would be considering the use of the ***.dropna()*** and ***.fillna()*** methods for removing and filling up missing data points respectively.

To illustrate this, we will create a data frame – to represent imported data with missing values, and then use these two data preparation methods on it.

Example: Another way to create a data frame is by using a dictionary. Remember, a python dictionary is somehow similar to a Pandas series in that they have key-value pairs, just as Pandas series are label-value pairs (although this is a simplistic comparison for the sake of conceptualization).

```
In []:# First, our dictionary
 dico = {'X':[1,2,np.nan],'Y':[4,np.nan,np.nan],'Z':[7,8,9]}
 dico #show

 # passing the dictionary to a dataframe
 row_labels = 'A B C'.split()
 df = pd.DataFrame(dico,row_labels)
 df #show
```

Output:

```
{'X': [1, 2, nan], 'Y': [4, nan, nan], 'Z': [7, 8, 9]}
```

	X	Y	Z
A	1.0	4.0	7
B	2.0	NaN	8
C	NaN	NaN	9

Now, let us start off with the ***.dropna()*** method. This removes any 'null' or 'nan' values in the data frame it's called off, either column-wise or row-wise, depending on the axis specification and other arguments passed to the method. It has the following default syntax:

```
df.dropna(axis=0, how='any', thresh=None, subset=None,
          inplace=False)
```

The 'df' above is the data frame name. The default axis is set to zero, which represent row-wise operation. Hence, at default, the method will remove any row containing 'nan' values.

Let us see what happens when we call this method for our data frame.

In []: # this removes 'nan' row-wise

df.dropna()

Output:

	X	Y	Z
A	1.0	4.0	7

Notice that rows B and C contain at least a 'nan' value. Hence, they were removed.

Let us try a column-wise operation by specifying the axis=1.

In []: # this removes 'nan' column-wise

df.dropna(axis=1)

Output:

	Z
A	7
B	8
C	9

As expected, only the column 'Z' was returned.

Now, in case we want to set a condition for a minimum number of 'non-nan' values/ actual data points required to make the cut (or escape the cut, depending on your perspective), we can use the 'thresh' (short for threshold) parameter to specify this.

Say, we want to remove 'nan' row-wise, but we only want to remove instances where the row had more than one actual data point value. We can set the threshold to 2 as illustrated in the following code:

```
In []: # drop rows with less than 2 actual values

       df.dropna(thresh = 2)
```

Output:

	X	Y	Z
A	1.0	4.0	7
B	2.0	NaN	8

Notice how we have filtered out row C, since it contains only one actual value '9'.

Exercise: Filter out columns in the data frame 'df' containing less than 2 actual data points

Next, let us use the ***.fillna()*** method to replace the missing values with our extrapolations.

Let us go ahead and replace our 'NaN' values with an 'x' marker. We can specify the 'X' as a string, and pass it into the 'value' parameter in ***.fillna()*.**

In []: # filling up NaNs

```
df.fillna('X')
```

Output:

	X	Y	Z
A	**1**	**4**	**7**
B	**2**	**X**	**8**
C	**X**	**X**	**9**

While marking missing data with an 'X' is fun, it is sometimes more intuitive (for lack of a better statistical approach), to use the mean of the affected column as a replacement for the missing elements.

Chapter 14. Group-By

This Pandas method, as the name suggests, allows the grouping of related data to perform combined/aggregate operations on them.

XYZ sales information

	Sales Person	Product	Sales
1	Sam	Hp	200
2	Charlie	Hp	120
3	Amy	Apple	340
4	Vanessa	Apple	124
5	Carl	Dell	243
6	Sarah	Dell	350

From our dataset, we can observe some common items under the product column. This is an example of an entry point for the group-by method in a data set. We can find information about the sales using the product grouping.

```
In []: # finding sales information by product

 print('Total items sold: by product')
 df.groupby('Product').sum()
```

Total items sold: by product

	Sales
Product	
Apple	**464**
Dell	**593**
Hp	**320**

This is an example of an aggregate operation using groupby. Other functions can be called to display interesting results as well. For example, ***.count()***:

In []: df.groupby('Product').count()

Output:

	Sales Person	Sales
Product		
Apple	**2**	**2**
Dell	**2**	**2**
Hp	**2**	**2**

While the previous operation could not return the 'Sales person' field, since a numeric operation like 'sum' cannot be performed on a string, the count method returns the instances of each product within both categories. Via this output, we can easily infer that XYZ company assigns two salespersons per product, and that each of the sales persons made a sale of the products. However, unlike the sum method, this count method does not give a clearer overview of the sales. This is why so many methods are usually called to explain certain aspects of data. A very useful method for checking multiple information at a time is the .describe() method.

```
In []: #Getting better info using describe ()

    df.groupby('Product').describe()
```

Output:

	Sales							
	count	mean	std	min	25%	50%	75%	max
Product								
Apple	2.0	232.0	152.735065	124.0	178.00	232.0	286.00	340.0
Dell	2.0	296.5	75.660426	243.0	269.75	296.5	323.25	350.0

Hp	**2.0**	**160.0**	**56.568542**	**120.0**	**140.0**	**160.0**	**180.0**	**200.0**

Now, this is more informative. It says a lot about the data at a glance. Individual products can also be selected: df.groupby('Product').describe()['Product name e.g. 'Apple'].

Chapter 15. Reading and writing data

In real-world applications, data comes in various formats. These are the most common ones: CSV, Excel spreadsheets (xlsx / xls), HTML and SQL. While Pandas can read SQL files, it is not necessarily the best for working with SQL databases, since there are quite a few SQL engines: SQL lite, PostgreSQL, MySQL, etc. Hence, we will only be considering CSV, Excel and HTML.

Read

The ***pd.read_file_type('file_name')*** method is the default way to read files into the Pandas framework. After import, pandas displays the content as a data frame for manipulation using all the methods we have practiced so far, and more.

CSV (comma separated variables) & Excel

Create a CSV file in excel and save it in your python directory. You can check where your python directory is in Jupyter notebook by typing: ***pwd().*** If you want to change to another directory containing your files (e.g. Desktop), you can use the following code:

```
In []: import os
 os.chdir('C:\\Users\\Username\\Desktop')
```

To import your CSV file, type: pd.read_csv('csv_file_name'). Pandas will automatically detect the data stored in the file and display it as a data frame. A better approach would be to assign the imported data to a variable like this:

```
In []:Csv_data = pd.read_csv('example file.csv')
```

```
Csv_data          # show
```

Running this cell will assign the data in 'example file.csv' to the variable Csv_data, which is of the type data frame. Now it can be called later or used for performing some of the data frame operations.

For excel files (.xlsx and .xls files), the same approach is taken. To read an excel file named 'class data.xlsx', we use the following code:

```
In []:Xl_data = pd.read_excel('class data.xlsx')
  Xl_data          # show
```

This returns a data frame of the required values. You may notice that an index starting from 0 is automatically assigned at the left side. This is similar to declaring a data frame without explicitly including the index field. You can add index names, like we did in previous examples.

Tip: in case the excel spreadsheet has multiple sheets filled. You can specify the sheet you need to be imported. Say we need only sheet 1, we use: ***sheetname = 'Sheet 1'***. For extra functionality, you may check the documentation for ***read_excel()*** by using ***shift+tab***.

Write

After working with our imported or pandas-built data frames, we can write the resulting data frame back into various formats. We will, however, only consider writing back to CSV and excel. To write a data frame to CSV, use the following syntax:

```
In []:Csv_data.to_csv('file name',index = False)
```

This writes the data frame 'Csv_data' to a CSV file with the specified filename in the python directory. If the file does not exist, it creates it.

For writing to an excel file, a similar syntax is used, but with sheet name specified for the data frame being exported.

```
In []:  Xl_data.to_excel('file name.xlsx',sheet_name = 'Sheet 1')
```

This writes the data frame ***Xl_data*** to sheet one of ***'file name.xlsx'***.

Html

Reading Html files through pandas requires a few libraries to be installed: htmllib5, lxml, and BeautifulSoup4. Since we installed the latest Anaconda, these libraries are likely to be included. Use ***conda list*** to verify, and ***conda install*** to install any missing ones.

Html tables can be directly read into pandas using the ***pd.read_html ('sheet url')*** method. The sheet url is a web link to the data set to be imported. As an example, let us import the 'Failed bank lists' dataset from FDIC's website and call it w_data.

```
In []: w_data = pd.read_html('http://www.fdic.gov/bank/individual/failed/banklist.html')


w_data[0]
```

To display the result, here we used ***w_data [0]***. This is because the table we need is the first sheet element in the webpage source code. If you are familiar with HTML, you can easily identify where each element lies. To inspect a web page source code, use Chrome browser. ***On the web page >> right click >> then, select 'view page source'***. Since what we are looking for is a table-like data, it will be specified like that in the source code. For example, here is where the data set is created in the FDIC page source code:

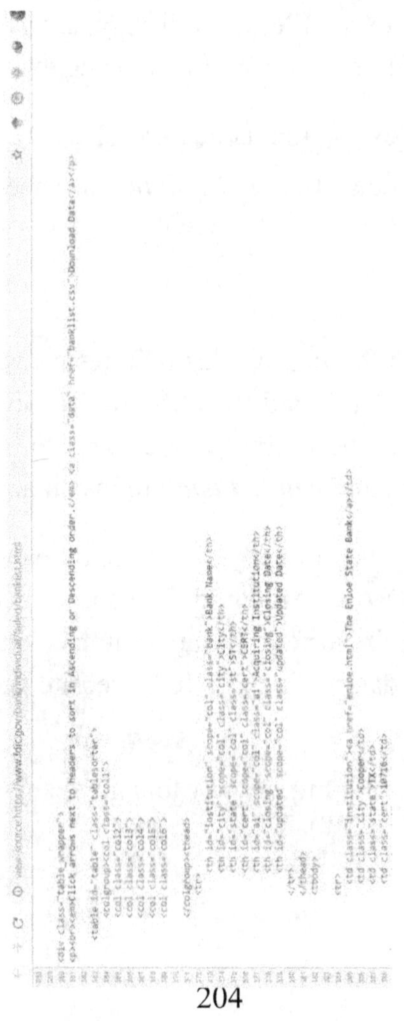

FDIC page source via chrome

This section concludes our lessons on the Pandas framework. To test your knowledge on all that has been introduced, ensure to attempt all the exercises below. In the next chapter, we will be exploring some data visualization frameworks.

For the exercise, we will be working on an example dataset. A salary spreadsheet from Kaggle.com. Go ahead and download the spreadsheet from this link: www.kaggle.com/kaggle/sf-salaries

Note: **You might be required to register before downloading the file.** Download the file to your python directory and extract the file.

Exercises: We will be applying all we have learned here.

1. Import pandas as pd

2. Import the CSV file into Jupyter notebook, assign it to a variable 'Sal', and display the first 5 values.
   Hint: *use the* **.head()** *method to display the first 5 values of a data frame. Likewise,* **.tail()** *is used for displaying the last 5 results. To specify more values, pass* ***'n=value'*** *into the method.*

3. What is the highest pay (including benefits)? Answer: 567595.43
   Hint: *Use data frame column indexing and* **.max()** *method.*

4. According to the data, what is 'MONICA FIELDS's Job title, and how much does she make plus benefits?

Answer: Deputy Chief of the Fire Department, and $ 261,366.14.

Hint: *Data frame column selection and conditional selection works (conditional selection can be found under Example 72. Use column index =='string' for the Boolean condition).*

5. Finally, who earns the highest basic salary (minus benefits), and by how much is their salary higher than the average basic salary. Answer: NATHANIEL FORD earns the highest. His salary is higher than the average by $ 492827.1080282971.

Hint: *Use the* **.max()**, *and* **.mean()** *methods for the pay gap. Conditional selection with column indexing also works for the employee name with the highest pay.*

Part 3: MACHINE LEARNING WITH PYTHON

Chapter 15. What is machine learning

This technological approach is radically different from the way companies traditionally exploit data. Instead of starting with business logic and applying the data, machine learning techniques allow data to create logic. One of the key benefits of this approach is the removal of commercial assumptions and prejudices that may lead managers to customize a strategy that may not be the best.

The different benefits that come with machine learning, it is time to move on and learn a bit more about some of the other things that you are going to be able to do with this as well. As you start to work with the process of machine learning a bit more, you will find that there are a lot of different ways that you are able to use it and many programmers are taking it to the next level to create things that are unique and quite fun.

Chapter 16. categories of machine learning

The Machine Learning algorithms can fall either in the supervised or unsupervised or reinforced learning.

Supervised Learning

For the case of supervised learning, the human is expected to provide both the inputs and the outputs which are desired and furnish the feedback based on the accuracy of the predictions during training. After completion of the training, the algorithm will have to apply what was applied to the next data.

The concept of supervised learning can be seen to be similar to learning under a teacher's supervision in human beings. The teacher gives some examples to the student, and the student then derives new rules and knowledge from these examples so as to apply this somewhere else.

It is also good for you to know the difference between the regression problems and classification problems. In regression problems, the target is a numeric value, while in classification; the target is a class or a tag. A regression task can help determine the average cost of all houses in London, while a classification task will help determine the types of flowers based on the length of their sepals and petals.

Unsupervised Learning

For the case of unsupervised learning, the algorithms do not expect to be provided with the output data. An approach called deep learning, which is an iterative approach, is used so as to review the data and arrive at new conclusions. This makes them suitable for use in processing tasks which are complex compared to the supervised learning algorithms. This means that the unsupervised learning algorithms learn solely from examples without responses to these. The algorithm finds patterns from the examples on its own.

Supervised learning algorithms work similarly to how humans determine any similarities between two or more objects. Majority of recommender systems you encounter when purchasing items online work based on unsupervised learning algorithms. In this case, the algorithm derives what to suggest to you for purchase from what you have purchased before. The algorithm has to estimate the kind of customers whom you resemble, and a suggestion is drawn from that.

Reinforcement Learning

This type of learning occurs when the algorithm is presented with examples which lack labels, as it is the case with unsupervised learning. However, the example can be accompanied by a positive or a negative feedback depending on the solution which is proposed by the algorithm. It is associated with applications in which the algorithm has to make decisions, and these decisions are associated with a consequence. It is similar to trial and error in human learning.

Errors become useful in learning when they are associated with a penalty such as pain, cost, loss of time etc. In reinforced learning, some actions are more likely to succeed compared to others.

Machine learning processes are similar to those of data mining and predictive modeling. In both cases, searching through the data is required so as to draw patterns then adjust the actions of the program accordingly. A good example of machine learning is the recommender systems. If you purchase an item online, you will get an ad which is related to that item, and that is a good example of machine learning.

Chapter 17. qualitative examples of machine learning applications

In statistical modeling, you might notice that reversion analysis aims to be a process which helps estimate the various relationships between different variables. This will include several techniques that are typically used for variable analysis and matching when several variables are worked with at once whenever you are showing the relationship between independent and dependent variables.

Reversion analysis is a valuable tool when it comes to understanding how the usual value for variable changes over time. Reversion will also help you estimate the conditional expectation of a variable that depends on the independent variable and the average value of said variable. Briefly put, it will shorten the time you spend while juggling multiple values.

More uncommon are situations where you will be presented with a variable that depends on the independent variable along with its quantile or location parameters for the conditional distribution. Usually, the estimate you come to will be an expression for the independent value. We call this the reversion expression. In reversion analysis, you will be showing your interest in the characterization of the variation of the dependent variable in relation to the expression which we can describe as the probability distribution.

One of the possible approaches is taking a conditional analysis. This will take the estimate for the maximum over the average for the dependent variables, which are, again, based on the independent variable that is given. This allows you to determine if the independent variable is necessary or sufficient for the value that the dependent variable holds.

You will use reversion when you are looking to forecast and when it overlaps with machine learning. It will be a good tool for when you are trying the relationships between dependent and independent variables. When dealing with a restricted circumstance, reversion will be used to infer the causal relationship between the variables. You should be cautious, however, as it may give you a false relationship.

There are several different techniques for reversion. Linear reversion and least squares diversion are two of them. Your reversion expression will be defined as finite numbers which don't have a parameter. Nonparametric reversion is a tool that we will be utilizing when we want to permit the reversion expression to be used as a collection of expressions for infinite dimensionality.

Your performance when it comes to revision analysis is going to be a summary of the methods that you practice as processes for data generation and how it ties back into the reversion approach that you applied. The true form of data generation is not always going to be known as reversion analysis and depends on the extent of your assumptions.

The assumptions you provide will need to be testable so you can see if you have provided the machine with enough data.

Machine Learning and Robotics

I believe that we have helped you grow more familiar with what machine learning is. It should not surprise you that it sparked an interest in robotics and has stayed roughly the same for the past several years. But are robots related to machine learning?

Robotics has not developed too much in the past several years. However, these developments are a great foundation for discoveries to come and some even relate to machine learning.

When it comes to robotics, the following five applications apply in machine learning:

1. **Computer vision:** some would say that robot vision and machine vision are more correct as far as terminology goes. For a very long time, engineers and roboticists have been trying to develop a type of camera that will let a robot process the physical world around him as data. Robot vision and machine vision are two terms that go hand in hand. Their creation can be credited to the existence of automated inspection systems and robot guidance. The two have a very small difference and it comes in regards to kinematics in the use of robot vision. It encompasses the calibration of the comment frame and enhances the robot's ability to affect its surroundings physically.

The already impressive advances in computer vision that have been instrumental in coming up with techniques that are geared for prediction learning, has been further helped by a huge influx of data.

2. **Imitation learning:** this is relatively closely connected to observational learning. It is common with kids and has common features, the most obvious being probabilistic models and Batesian. The main question, however, stands. Will it find use in humanoid robots?

Imitation learning has always been an important part of robotics as it has features of mobility that transcend those of factory settings in domains like search and rescue construction, which makes the programming robotic solutions manually a puzzle.

3. **Self-Supervised learning:** Allows robots to generate their training instance due to the self-supervised learning approaches, in order to improve their performance. This includes priority training, as well as data that is captured and is used to translate vague sensor data. The robots with optical devices that have this installed can reject and detect objects.

A solid example called Watch-Bot has been created by Cornell and Stanford. It utilized a laptop and laser pointer, a 3D sensor, and a camera in order to find normal human activities like patterns that are learned through the methods of probability. A laser pointer is used to detect the distance to the object. Humans are notified 60 percent of the time, as the robot has no concept of what he is doing and why he is doing it.

4. **Medical and assistive technologies:** A device that senses and oversees the processing of sensory information before setting an action that is going to benefit a senior or someone with incapacities. This is the basic definition of the assistive robot. They have a capacity for movement therapy, as well as the ability to provide other therapeutic and diagnostic benefits. They are quite cost-prohibitive for hospitals in the US and abroad, so they still haven't left the lab.

Robotics in the field of medicine has advanced at a rapid rate even though they are not used by medical facilities. This advancement can be seen clearly if you see the capabilities of these robots.

5. **Multi-Agent learning:** It offers some key components such as negotiation and coordination. This involves that the robot, based on machine learning, finds equilibrium strategies and adapts to a shifting landscape.

During late 2014, an excellent example of an algorithm used by distributed robots or agents was made in one of MIT's labs for decision and information systems. The robots collaborated and opted to build a more inclusive and better learning model than that which was done by a single robot. They did so via building exploration and teaching them to find the quickest ways through the rooms in order to construct a knowledge base in an autonomous manner.

Chapter 18. python and machine learning

Have you been using the classification as a type of machine learning? Probably yes, even if you did not know about it. Example: The email system has the ability to automatically detect spam. This means that the system will analyze all incoming messages and mark them as spam or non-spam.

Often, you, as an end user, have the option to manually tag messages as spam, to improve the ability to detect spam. This is a form of machine learning where the system takes the examples of two types of messages: spam and so-called ham (the typical term for "non-spam email") and using these cases automatically classify incoming mails fetched.

What is a classification? Using the examples from the same domain of the problem belonging to the different classes of the model train or the "generate rules" which can be applied to (previously unknown) examples.

Dataset Iris is a classic collection of data from the 1930s; This is one of the first examples of modern statistical classifications. These measurements allow us to identify the different types of flower.

Today, the species are identified through DNA, but in the 30s the role of DNA in genetics had not yet been recorded. Four characteristics were selected for each plant sepal length (length of cup slip) sepal width (width of cup slip) petal length, and petal width. There are three classes that identify the plant: Iris setosa, Iris versicolor, and Iris virginica.

Formulation of the problem

This dataset has four characteristics. In addition, each plant species was recorded, as well as the value of class characteristics. The problem we want to solve is: Given these examples, can we anticipate a new type of flower in the field based on measurements?

This is the problem of classification or supervised learning, where based on the selected data, we can "generate rules" that can later be applied to other cases. Examples for readers who do not study botany are: filtering unwanted email, intrusion detection in computer systems and networks, detection of fraud with credit cards, etc.

Data Visualization will present a kind of triangle, circle type, and virginica type of mark x.

The model has already discussed a simple model that achieves 94% accuracy on the entire data set. The data we use to define what would be the threshold was then used to estimate the model.

What I really want to do is to assess the ability of generalization model. In other words, we should measure the performance of the algorithm in cases where classified information, which is not trained, is used.

Transmitting device stringent evaluation and use the "delayed" (Casually, Held-out) data is one way to do this.

However, the accuracy of the test data is lower! While this may surprise an inexperienced person who is engaged in machine learning, it's expected to be lower by veterans. Generally, the accuracy of testing is lower than the accuracy of training. Using the previous examples you should be able to plot a graph of this data. The graph will show the boundary decisions.

Consider what would happen if the decision to limit some of the cases near the border were not there during the training? It is easy to conclude that the boundaries move slightly to the right or left.

NOTES: In this case, the difference between the accuracy of the measured data for training and testing is not great. When using a complex model, it is possible to get 100% accuracy in training and very low accuracy testing! In other words, the accuracy of the training set is a too optimistic assessment of how good your algorithm is. Experiments always measured and reported the accuracy of testing and accuracy on the set of examples that are not being used for the training!

A possible problem with the hold-out validation is that we are only using half of the data used for training. However, if you use too much data for training, assessment error testing is done on a very small number of examples. Ideally, we would use all the data for the training and all the data for testing, but it was impossible.

A good approximation of the impossible ideals is a method called cross-validation. The simplest form of cross-validation is Leave-one-out cross-validation.

When using cross-checking, each example was tested on a model trained without taking into account that data. Therefore, cross-validation is a reliable estimate of the possibilities of generalization model. The main problem with the previous method of validation is a need for training of a large number (the number grows to the size of the set).

Instead, let's look at the so-called v-fold validation. If, for example, using 5-fold cross-validation, the data is divided into five parts, of which in each iteration 4 parts are used for training and one for testing.

The number of parts in the initial set of components depends on the size of the event, the time required for the training model, and so on. When generating fold data, it is very important to be balanced.

Chapter 19. machine learning and data science,

You may also start to notice that there are many different companies, from startups to more established firms, that are working with machine learning because they love what it is able to do to help their business grow. There are so many options when it comes to working with machine learning, but some of the ones that you may use the most often are going to include:

- Statistical research: machine learning is a big part of IT now. You will find that machine learning will help you to go through a lot of complexity when looking through large data patterns. Some of the options that will use statistical research include search engines, credit cards, and filtering spam messages.

- Big data analysis: many companies need to be able to get through a lot of data in a short amount of time. They use this data to recognize how their customers spend money and even to make decisions and predictions about the future. This used to take a long time to have someone sit through and look at the data, but now machine learning can do the process faster and much more efficiently. Options like election campaigns, medical fields, and retail stores have used machine learning for this purpose.

- Finances: some finance companies have also used machine learning. Stock trading online has seen a rise in the use of machine learning to help make efficient and safe decisions and so much more.

As we have mentioned above, these are just three of the ways that you are able to apply the principles of machine learning in order to get the results that you want to aid in your business or even to help you create a brand new program that works the way that you want. As technology begins to progress, even more, you will find that new applications and ideas for how this should work are going to grow as well.

Chapter 20. model validation

Data modeling is an important aspect of Data Science. It is one of the most rewarding processes that receive the most attention among learners of Data Science. However, things aren't the same as they might look because there is so much to it rather than applying a function to a given class of package.

The biggest part of Data Science is assessing a model to make sure that it is strong and reliable. In addition, Data Science modeling is highly associated with building information feature set. It involves different processes which make sure that the data at hand is harnessed in the best way.

Robust Data Model

Robust data models are important in creating the production. First, they must have better performance depending on different metrics. Usually, a single metric can mislead the way a model performs because there are many aspects in the classification problems.

Sensitivity analysis describes another important aspect of Data Science modeling. This is something that is important for testing a model to make sure it is strong. Sensitivity refers to a condition which the output of a model is meant to change considerably if the input changes slightly. This is very undesirable because it must be checked since the robust model is stable.

Lastly, interpretability is an essential aspect even though it is not always possible. This is usually related to how easy one can interpret the results of a model. But most modern models resemble black boxes. This makes it hard for one to interpret them. Besides that, it is better to go for an interpretable model because you might need to defend the output from others.

How Featurization Is Achieved

For a model to work best, it must require information that has a rich set of features. The latter is developed in different ways. Whichever the case, cleaning the data is a must. This calls for fixing issues with the data points, filling missing values where it is possible and in some situations removing noisy elements.

Before the variables are used in a model, you must perform normalization on them. This is achieved using a linear transformation on making sure that the variable values rotate around a given range. Usually, normalization is enough for one to turn variables into features once they are cleaned.

Binning is another process which facilitates featurization. It involves building nominal variables which can further be broken down into different binary features applied in a data model.

Lastly, some reduction methods are important in building a feature set. This involves building a linear combination of features that display the same information in fewer dimensions.

Important Considerations

Besides the basic attributes of Data Science modeling, there are other important things that a Data Scientist must know to create something valuable. Things such as in-depth testing using specialized sampling, sensitivity analysis, and different aspects of the model performance to improve a given performance aspect belong to Data Science modeling.

Chapter 21. machine learning case studies

To help you understand just how deep the field of deep learning goes and just how much it has changed everyone's lives already, I will dedicate this section to showing you specific examples of deep learning and how it is used in its myriad of applications.

Keep in mind, this is not meant to advertise any kind of product or service, but to show you that deep learning is far more common than many people think and that it is not a field pertaining to the higher levels of each industry, but one that belongs to all of us to some extent.

So, without further ado, let's dive in:

Image Curation on Yelp

Although Yelp may not be as popular as it used to be, it still has a very important role to play in how people experience the new places in their living areas (or the different locations they visit as tourists, for example).

At first, Yelp may seem like anything but a tech company - but they are using actual machine learning to make sure their users come back to the site because it provides them with actual, helpful information.

More specifically, Yelp has developed a machine learning system capable of classifying, categorizing, and labeling images submitted by users - but more importantly, this system helps Yelp do this in a genuinely efficient way. This is extremely important for the company, given the huge amounts of image data they receive every day.

Pinterest Content

Who knew searching for wedding ideas on Pinterest is fueled by machine learning?

Pinterest's main purpose is that of curating existing content - so it makes all the sense in the world that they have invested in machine learning to make this process faster and more accurate for their users.

The system developed by Pinterest is capable of moderating spam and helping users find content that is more relevant to their own interests, their styles, and their searches.

Facebook's Chatbots

By this point, it is more than likely that you have stumbled upon at least one chatbot in Facebook Messenger.

These apparently simplistic chatbots are, in fact, a form of primordial artificial intelligence. Sure, Skynet is not typing from the other end of the communication box, but even so, chatbots are a fascinating sub-field of artificial intelligence - one that is developing quite steadily.

Facebook Messenger allows any developer to create and submit their own chatbots. This is incredibly helpful for a variety of companies that emphasize their customer service and retention, because these chatbots can be used for this precise purpose. Sometimes, Messenger chatbots are so well-built that you may not even realize that you are talking to a, "robot."

Aside from chatbots, Facebook invests a lot in developing AI tools capable of reading images to visually impaired people, tools capable of filtering out spam and bad content, and so on.

In some ways, a company that might not seem to have a lot to do with technological innovation is pushing the boundaries of one of the most exciting fields of the tech world: artificial intelligence.

Google's Dreamy Machines

Google is one of the companies constantly investing in artificial intelligence (often, with amazing results). Not only have they developed translation systems based on machine learning, but pretty much every area of their activity is somewhat related to artificial intelligence too.

Don't be fooled - Google has its hands in much more than search engines. In recent years, they have invested a lot in a very wide range of industries, including medical devices, anti-aging tech, and, of course, neural networks.

The DeepMind network is, by far, one of the most impressive neural network research projects ran by Google. This network has been dubbed as the "machine that dreams" when images recreated by it were released to the public, opening everyone's eyes to how artificial intelligence, "perceives" the world.

Baidu Voice Search

Since China is the leading country in artificial intelligence research, it only makes sense that their leading search company, Baidu, is heavily invested in the realm of artificial intelligence too.

One of the most notable examples here is their voice search system which is already capable of mimicking human speech in a way that makes it undistinguishable form, well, **actual** human speech.

IBM's Watson

We couldn't have missed Watson from this list, mostly because this is one of the first impressively successful artificial intelligence endeavors in history.

Most people know IBM's Watson from its participation in **Jeopardy!**, but the supercomputer built by the super tech giant IBM can do **much** more than just compete in televised shows.

In fact, Watson has proved to be very useful to hospitals, helping them propose better treatment in some cancer cases. Given the paramount importance of this type of activity in medicine, it can be said that Watson helps to save actual lives - which is a truly great example of how AI can serve mankind.

Salesforce's Smart CRM

Salesforce is one of the leading tech companies, specifically in the field of sales and marketing, where the tool helps businesses maximize their sales potential and close more deals with their customers.

Salesforce is based on a machine learning tool that can predict leads and assigns scores for each of them. For sales people and marketing pros, this is a true gold mine because it makes the entire sale process smoother, more fluent, and, overall, more efficient.

Where Do You Come From, Where Do You Go, Deep Learning?

Clearly, deep learning advances are quite fascinating. Many take them for granted simply because the speed at which they have developed in recent years means that every year brings a new tool to the market - a tool to use in medicine, healthcare, business, commerce, and more.

The future of deep learning cannot be predicted with certainty - if we had an ultra-powerful AI, it might be able to make an accurate prediction of what will happen next. Even so, **human brains** figure that the following will happen over the next few years:

Better Learning

The more they learn, the more powerful machines become. We have a long way to go before we see the first full AI that is capable of mimicking thought processes and emotions - but the more AI is learning, the faster it will continue to grow.

As I was saying earlier in this book, it is a snowballing effect - so the more the "machine learning ball" is rolling, the larger it will become, and the more strength it will have.

Better Cyber Attack Protection

While humans might be able to beat codes created by humans, it might be a little more difficult for hackers to break in when an AI is protecting the realms of data held by a company. Soon enough, artificial intelligence will be capable of better monitoring, prevention, and responses when it comes to database breaches, DDoS attacks, and other cyberthreats.

Better Generative Models

Generative models aim to mimic human beings as much as they can, in very specific areas. The Baidu example in the previous section is a very good indicator here. Over the next few years, we will start to see a lot more of these very convincing generative models, to the point where we will not be able to make a clear distinction between humans and machines (at least in some respects).

Better Training for Machines

Machine learning training is fairly new, given the rapid ascension of this industry in the past couple of decades. The more we train our machines, however, the better we will become at it - and this means that the machines themselves will be able to make better, more accurate decisions.

Part 4 : WORKBOOK

So far we've discussed the theoretical and technical aspects of data science and machine learning, but there is one more addition to your skillset that needs to be addressed, and that's visualization. Creating visualizations with Python is vital for any aspiring data scientist because it can easily enrich a project and communicate information a lot more clearly and efficiently.

Visualization involves the use of plots, graphics, tables, interactive charts, and much more. Viewing data through an artistic representation helps users greatly in analyzing it because, let's face it, looking at colorful charts makes things clearer than endless strings of numbers that tire your eyes. Visualization helps with operations that involve data comparisons, complex measurements, or identifying patterns.

The basics of visualization and explore tools such as matplotlib and bokeh. Knowing how to efficiently communicate information to others is a crucial skill, and even though you are only at the beginning of your journey, you should get an idea of the concepts and tools behind visualization.

Matplotlib

Since visualization is a complex topic that requires its own book, we are going to stick to the basics of using Python to create various graphic charts.

So what is matplotlib? It is basically a Python package that is designed for plotting graphics. It was created because there was little to no integration between the programming language and other tools designed specifically for graphical representations. If you already became familiar with MATLAB, you might notice that the syntax is very similar. That's because this package was heavily influenced by MATLAB and the module we are going to focus on is fully compatible with it. The "matplotlib.pyplot" module will be the core of this basic introduction to visualization.

Creating, improving, and enriching your graphical representation is easy with plypot commands, because with this module you can make changes to instantiated figures. Now let's go through some examples and discuss the basic guidelines that will allow you to create your own visualization draft.

First, you need to import all the modules and packages by typing the following lines in Python:

In: import numpy as np

import matplotlib.pyplot as plt

import matplotlib as mpl

Now let's start by first drawing a function. This is the most basic visualization, as it requires only a series of x coordinates that are mapped on the y axis. This is known as a **curve representation** because the results are stored in two vectors. Keep in mind that the precision of the visual representation depends on the number of mapping points

But what if we want to visualize our data by using a histogram? Histograms are one of the best visualization methods when we want to clearly see how variables are distributed. Let's create an example where we have two distributions with standard deviation.

Interactive Visualization

Interactive visualization that is processed inside a browser became very popular due to the success of D3.js, which is a JavaScript library used for creating web-based data visualization with interactive features. This tool is preferred over other methods because there is no latency, meaning data is delivered fast, and visualization can be personalized in many ways.

For Python, we have a similar tool to D3.js called Bokeh (a Japanese term used in photography). This can be found as a component of the pydata stack and is fully interactive, customizable, and efficient. The creation of visual representation methods that are otherwise complex and time consuming for the data scientist. With Bokeh, you can create interactive plots, dashboards, charts, and other visual representations that can handle even large data sets.

For the purposes of this book, we are going to discuss this topic only briefly and focus on matplotlib-based plots. Feel free to explore this tool on your own, because it is intuitively designed with the user in mind and the documentation for it is plentiful.

We create an html file and upload it to the browser. If you used Jupyter until this point, keep in mind that this kind of interactive visualization won't work with it due to our output preference, which is the output_file. Now you can use any website to incorporate the output. Next, you will notice that there are various tools on the right side of the plot. These tools allow you to personalize the chart by enlarging it, and manipulating it with dragging and scrolling. Bokeh is an interactive tool that can be integrated with other packages as well. If you become familiar with tools such as Seaborn or ggplot, you can transfer the visual representation from them into Bokeh. The method used to achieve this is "to_bokeh" and it simply ports charts from other visualization tools. You can also use pandas functions together with Bokeh, such as data conversions.

Quiz

1. When is it Right to Apply Machine Learning?
2. Why is Machine Learning important?
3. Big Data? How does it matter?
4. Why Security Data Science?
5. What is the Reason for Increased Ransom ware Attacks and Data Breaches?

Answers

1. When you are about to work on a complex task or issue, that is the perfect time to apply Machine Learning.

2. An increase in Big Data makes Machine Learning an essential method to solve problems such as:

- Image processing and computer vision
- Energy production for load forecasting
- Computational finance for algorithmic trading and credit scoring
- Natural language processing to help recognize a voice
- Aerospace, automotive, and manufacturing for predictive maintenance

3. Big Data describes data sets that have a size that surpass the normal function of database software tools such as storage, capturing, and analyzing.

It refers to a collection of data sets that are very large and complex such that one cannot process using simple database management tools.

4. This is focused on upgrading information security via practical applications of Statistics, Data Analysis, Machine Learning, and Data Visualization. While the tools and techniques are not different compared to those applied in Data Science, this field has a major focus on decreasing risk and identification of fraud.

5. There are quite a number of reasons to explain the rise in ransom ware attacks and data breaches:

- Attackers discover an efficient way to generate quick cash using ransom ware. One reason for this is that you can find ransom ware as a service on the dark Web. As a result, attackers can choose to leverage on the ransom ware service and concentrate on the ransom extortion.
- The attack surface has increased, and the network perimeter is dissolved as a result of cloud and mobile.
- Attackers have increased the number of tools as a means to escape the current information security tools.
- The information security team has insufficient cameras to monitor movements of an intruder in the network enterprise. Therefore, adversaries have an advantage because they can move in any direction within the network of an enterprise.

Conclusion

Without any trace of doubt, machine learning and deep learning are two of the most exciting and interesting fields of study at the moment.

There are, truly, a million reasons to love artificial intelligence in general:

1. It is mankind's offspring
2. It brings together multiple disciplines
3. It improves productivity and efficiency
4. It is torn out of a SF movie (and yes, this might actually be a reason for some)

There are a lot of reasons to fear the advent of the AI era as well - starting with the fact that it comes with serious ethical implications and ending with the fact that nobody can tell you just how far AI will go and how, "sentient" it will become.

The book at hand did not aim to be a manual in Python or programming or even deep learning in general - but an incursion into the **realm** of these subjects, a short trip to make you curious about what Python and deep learning are all about, why they are used in association, and even **how** they are used, at times.

I know you will take the information presented here and use it to the best of your abilities, helping yourself create the future you want for your children, nephews, or simply neighbors.

Because, yes, as a data programmer, you belong to the future just as much as robots do. It means that even if everything in the world will be automated, your skills might still be needed. And it's great news from the point of view of the job satisfaction you get as well - because who doesn't love being useful and creating something as awesome as machines that are capable to save lives, predict financial situations, or simply make entertainment...more entertaining?

My purpose with this entire book was to show you that although deep learning is a truly intricate subject and that there is **a lot** to it, you can still be part of it if you put your mind to it. Python programming is, as I have repeatedly said it throughout the book, one of the easiest types of programming you can learn.

Its intuitive nature and the fact that you don't have to know how to program in more, "elevated" languages make it a truly beginner-friendly programming language even for people who have not written a line of code in their entire lives.

So, if you are interested in the realm of deep learning and the fascinating innovations it brings to the table, if you want a job that is future-proof or if you simply want to take on a challenge you will always remember, Python is for you. Even more, Python for deep learning is for you too, even if you have zero experience in programming.

Hopefully, I managed to instill curiosity in you - by showing you how simple Python can be, by showing you what artificial intelligence is all about, and by showing you clear examples of how AI is used in everyday applications without you even knowing about it.

Maybe even more importantly, I hope I helped you understand that AI and deep learning are not evil (or at least not inherently so), and that there are important ethical issues we should all discuss before it's too late in any way.

There are, of course, many other things that could have been discussed, beginning with the actual intricacies of Python and ending with newly arising ethical issues. What I meant to do is cover the very basics: the things you should absolutely know when you start showing an interest in this amazing field of science.

Because, yes, deep learning is a science by this point. It may have been fiction at the beginning of the 20th century and it may have been seen as delusional towards the middle of the same century but today, in 2019, deep learning is as real as it gets.

Artificial intelligence is, without the slightest trace of doubt, the final frontier in man-made computational sciences. It is the ultimate goal - the one that might help us live longer and happier, the one that might help us find a solution to the fact that we cannot exceed the speed of light, the one to help mankind make decisions based not on emotions and hunches, but on raw data.

Sure, this comes with its downfalls, as it was discussed in the last chapter of this book.

But if you are ready to embrace it all, you are ready to face the future with the largest possible smile on your face.

If you are ready to embrace Python even as a complete beginner, you are a daring soul who deserves to be part of the amazing future we're building in this industry.

If you are ready to embrace deep learning not just as a mere user, but as a programmer lying behind the inner works of these neural networks, you are a true pioneer in the grand scheme of things.

Hopefully, my book here has instilled all these sentiments in you - and it has made you ask all the important questions too.

What's next?

Get down and dirty with Python, learn its basics, and start coding. Just like riding a bike, writing programs for machine learning cannot happen without those first awkward steps - so stay optimistic, erase, try again, erase again, and then try once more.

The future is at your fingertips.

Use it wisely!

Python Programming

The 21 Best Tips and Tricks You Must Know To Approach Python Programming In The Right Way

#2020 Updated Version | Effective Computer Programming | Step by Step Explanations

Steve Tudor

Legal & Disclaimer

The information contained in this book and its contents is not designed to replace or take the place of any form of medical or professional advice; and is not meant to replace the need for independent medical, financial, legal or other professional advice or services, as may be required. The content and information in this book has been provided for educational and entertainment purposes only.

The content and information contained in this book has been compiled from sources deemed reliable, and it is accurate to the best of the Author's knowledge, information and belief. However, the Author cannot guarantee its accuracy and validity and cannot be held liable for any errors and/or omissions. Further, changes are periodically made to this book as and when needed. Where appropriate and/or necessary, you must consult a professional (including but not limited to your doctor, attorney, financial advisor or such other professional advisor) before using any of the suggested remedies, techniques, or information in this book.

Upon using the contents and information contained in this book, you agree to hold harmless the Author from and against any damages, costs, and expenses, including any legal fees potentially resulting from the application of any of the information provided by this book. This disclaimer applies to any loss, damages or injury caused by the use and application, whether directly or indirectly, of any advice or information presented, whether for breach of contract, tort, negligence, personal injury, criminal intent, or under any other cause of action.

You agree to accept all risks of using the information presented inside this book.

You agree that by continuing to read this book, where appropriate and/or necessary, you shall consult a professional (including but not limited to your doctor, attorney, or financial advisor or such other advisor as needed) before using any of the suggested remedies, techniques, or information in this book.

Introduction

Today computers are everywhere. Offices, homes, schools, departmental stores, everywhere we look, we find computers in one form or the other. In today's world there is no escaping the use of these machines. We use them to search for information, performing complex calculations, storing data, paying bills, human capital optimizations etc. Why these machines are so popular? The answer is simple and straight forward. Computers help us in day to day life, they make things easier and straight forward for us.

However, on their own these machines are unable to do anything. People tell them exactly what to do and they follow the instructions. These instructions that tell computers what to do are called computer programs and people who write these programs are called computer programmers or software engineers.

What is programming?

Now as we have established that computers follow instructions, the question arises how do we make computers understand what we want to tell them and in what language do we give the computers instructions.

Computers understand instructions written in special languages. Programs that are written in these languages give computers an exact sequence of steps to follow and the computer will follow these instructions without questioning or asking anything. Here we must mention that in our everyday life many times we give instructions to fellow human beings but we take certain things for granted thinking that people will automatically do some in between steps. For example, if a teacher asks a student sitting in his classroom to bring a book from the library he will give a single line instruction to bring such and such book from the library. However, there are several intermediate steps involved to carry out this instruction. The following sequence give the exact detail about how to carry out this instruction.

1. **Stand up from the chair.**
2. **Go out of the class room.**
3. **Turn left.**
4. **When you reach the library ask permission to enter.**
5. **Look for the book in the respective section.**
6. **Pull out the book.**
7. **Check out the book by informing the librarian.**
8. **Go back to the classroom.**
9. **Handover the book to the teacher.**

Hence you see that a single one line instruction requires a detailed process that we do not need to explain to people because they already know the intermediate steps but the case is different with computers. We have to tell them every single detail. Even in this case there may be some scenarios when the computer would block out our working because we have omitted the details like what if the book is not on the shelf or what if the librarian does not grant the student permission to enter the library. These small details are what we need to cater to while writing computer programs because computers do not have insight like humans. They cannot make any decisions like if one book is not available take another one that is similar to the one required, which can serve the same purpose. We make decisions for the computers. A good computer program will look for all the arcs that might stem from a decision point and write instructions for each case. The instructions are written in special computer understandable languages called programming languages.

Types of programming languages

There are numerous languages in which programmers write the instructions or code that would make computers do useful tasks. One might argue that why is there not one single language that tells the computer to do different tasks which could save the programmers from the hassle of learning so many different languages. The truth is that the computer understands everything by breaking it into a singular machine understandable binary code.

With the advancement in technology there are so many different ways in which we can program our machines and get benefit from them. Different languages are written keeping in view certain functionalities. However, recently languages are written keeping in mind ease of learning for the programmers. Such that programmers may feel like giving out instructions in the same way as to any other fellow human. This makes programming much easier.

There are three groups in which we can divide the computer languages.

High level programming languages

High level languages are similar to normal human languages. They are easier to understand and to program in. languages like C, C++, COBOL, fall in this category while our case study PYTHON is also a high level programming language. A program written in high level language is called a source code. A computer cannot understand the source code by itself. It needs special programs that translates the source code into machine understandable instructions. A compiler is a program that translates a high level language into a machine code. To the compiler a source program is just input data. The output that it generates against the input is called an object program. Object program is the machine language version of the program. However, a **compiler** needs an entire file of source code and it parses it as a whole, on the other hand an **interpreter** is another translator program that parses the source code line by line. Python is an interpreter program and does not follow the boilerplate model.

The main advantage of code written in high level language is that it is portable. It can run on any machine given that the machine has a proper compiler program that understands the specific source code.

Low Level Programming Language

A low level programming language is closer to machine code. Here instructions are represented as mnemonics. For example, typical instructions for addition and subtraction would look like following in a low level language like Assembly language.

ADD

SUB

Although languages like assembly is a difficult, it gives users more power to manipulate the machine according to his requirements. An assembler is a program that is used to translate instructions written in assembly language and convert it to machine code.

Machine Language

When computers were first developed the only programming language available was the primitive instruction set built into each machine called the machine code. The machine code is not similar on every computer.

The word bit that will often be used in programming refers to a single 0 or 1. A group of four bits is called a nibble. It is a pattern of 0's and 1's in a group of fours, but nibbles are very seldom used nowadays. A byte is a group of 8 bits. It can represent 2 to the power of 8 that is 256 combinations. In a computer each character is represented by a byte. However, now 8 bit computers are being replaced by 16 or 32 bit computers.

Working with binary combinations is a tedious process and fortunately nowadays we no longer work in it. Instead we use high level languages like Python with a language translator that would convert our instructions into machine code.

Phases of programming

Now that we have come to know about what computer programs are and how they are written, let us learn the process of writing a computer program. A computer program should be written in a systematic sequence of steps.

It all starts with a problem. We are given a situation and we have to find a programmable solution to it. it involves basically three main phases.

Problem solving phase

- Analysis and specification of the problem
- Developing an algorithm or sequence of steps to the solution.
- Verification of the algorithm.

Implementation Phase

- Translating the algorithm into a program.
- Testing the program for various test cases.

Maintenance Phase

- Using the program by end users.
- Modify the program according to the changing requirements and correct any errors that may occur.

Now let us discuss a little detail about algorithms. The process of writing a program begins by analyzing the problem and developing a general solution called an algorithm. It is highly advisable to spend a good amount of time analyzing the problem and developing the right algorithm before actually implementing the solution. This will ultimately save time and save a lot of effort later. Although a person is usually tempted to start writing the code immediately, in the long run it will end up in developing an erroneous code and would require a lot of time and effort to identify the errors and fix the bugs.

Translating an algorithm into a programming language is called coding the algorithm. The product of this translation is called a program. Running this program on a computer is called an execution. During the execution a number of errors and bugs can occur. That is when we use the concept of debugging. Debugging is basically tracking and removing errors from a program.

After a program is successfully executed and deployed on a computer machine it proceeds to the maintenance phase. In this phase whenever errors are reported by the client by testing with the real data, it needs to be fixed by modifying the program. A nicely written program that follows the general rules and good programming practices is easy to modify and update. That is why it is highly advisable to write the program following all the good practices that will be mentioned in this book as we move on to the next chapters.

Maintenance is also required once the requirements change or data is modified. For example, the program for a supermarket must provide provisions for an increase in the number of the items, changing prices, updates in sales tax.

Now that we are familiar with the general concepts, let us move on to learning about Python.

Chapter 1 : how to use this book

There are a lot of reasons you may want to Python. Or, you may just be looking for a place to start with the wide, wide world of programming. Regardless of your specific purpose and goal, I can guarantee you that the Python programming language will provide you with all of the tools that you need to do exactly what it is that you want to do.

If you're browsing the introductory pages of this book on a preview or something of the like, on the fence as to whether or not you want to learn Python, well, I can tell you that you probably should.

Why?

Well, Python is basically an incredibly useful and powerful language. It's present essentially everywhere. Everything from the scripting side of video games (or the video games themselves) to intensive server-side web applications to the plethora of deep and responsive desktop applications that have been built with it.

When should you use Python? The answer depends upon exactly what you're going to do. But since you're a beginner, I say you should learn anyway.

As you continue to grow as a programmer after this book, you're going to learn when you should and shouldn't use Python just as a matter of intuition. Python is an absolutely fantastic language, but the place where it fails is when you have to get extremely close to a computer's hardware or write incredibly efficient programs. In these areas, Python doesn't excel.

However, that's not to say it doesn't have its perks. In fact, I'd say that's one of the few places that Python falls flat. And what it lacks there, it makes up for in other areas. For example, development time in Python is generally extremely low in comparison to other languages. This is super easy to illustrate. Compare the following excerpts of code, the first from C++, the second from Java, and the last from Python.

Here's the C++ example:

```
#include <iostream>

using namespace std;

int main() {

print "Hello world" <<endl;

}
```

Here's the Java example:

```
public class javaExample {

public static void main(String args[]) {

System.out.println("Hello world\n");

}

}
```

And here's the Python example, for comparison:

```
print "Hello world\n"
```

See how much easier it is? And this is just with rudimentary programming concepts. When you get into heavier programming concepts like variables, functions, and other things of that nature, Python actually goes out of the way to make them really simple and functional to handle. We'll get more into this in the other chapters, of course.

On top of this, Python, as I've already said, is a language which has endless opportunity for usage and growth. There are very few explicitly **bad** situations for Python. This makes it a great language to learn initially for the simple fact that you'll be able to get a ton of mileage out of it. There will be very few times where, as a beginning programmer, you'll come up with a concept you'd like to carry out that you **won't** be able to conquer perfectly well with Python.

So enough of all that, how do we get started with Python? Well, you're going to need a few things first. Of course, you're going to need a computer, preferably with an active internet connection, but there are going to be more things that you need.

Let's start our programming adventure right here. I'm going to teach you everything that you need to get going with Python, so just follow along.

The first thing that you're going to need to grab is Python itself. You can get it by going to the Python website at http://python.org. You'll be able to download and install it for your respective operating system. Note that this isn't entirely relevant if you're working on Linux or macOS. Most versions of these operating systems will generally have a version of Python on it. You may, though, need to downgrade. If so, you're going to need to search for instructions which are relevant to your specific operating system because the instructions can vary depending upon which operating system you're using.

If you don't know whether Python is pre-installed or not, you can figure it out by going to either the Terminal (in macOS or Linux systems) or elevated Powershell (in Windows) and running the command "python". If your instance of Terminal or Powershell says something along the lines of "Command not recognized", then congratulations, you need to install Python. If it recognizes the command and says "Python 3.x.x" in the program initiation text, you need to downgrade.

Anyhow, on the Python site, you need to be certain that you're getting Python version 2.7.12, and **not** Python version 3. This is for one simple reason: Python 2 and 3 are a bit different in the way that they handle certain core functions. Not glaringly so, but one of the reasons that someone learns to program is so that they can speak directly to the computer. Learning Python 2 will give you many more opportunities to do this. This is for the simple reason that it's been **around** longer. There's much more code written for Python 2 than Python 3. You'll be able to work with a lot more code if you learn to work with Python 3 first. Now, granted, Python 3 is of course bleeding edge. But when you're learning to program, bleeding edge is not always best. It's preferable here that you learn how to read and write and deal with more code than you would otherwise. Basically, you're trying to cover as much ground with as little as possible when you're starting out, and Python 2 accommodates you for that goal perfectly. The few things you'll have to learn or relearn for Python 3 once you're more experienced with Python or programming in general will be non-factors compared to trying to understand deprecated code samples from Python 2 which aren't relevant to the code that you're trying to write.

With that out of the way, once you have Python 2.7.13 (or the latest version of Python 2 available) installed, you're going to need to get a text editor. It doesn't matter exactly what text editor you use, there are several good different candidates. The one I specifically recommend to use is called Atom, and you can get it at http://atom.io. There are a few reasons that I recommend this one. Firstly, it's free. What's better than high quality free software? Secondly, it's super simple to use and jam packed with features right out of the box, yet without being a sort of bloated and ugly software. Thirdly, it's incredibly extensible: there's nigh endless support for it through various different extensions and things of the sort online. There's so much that you can do with Atom. The endless possibilities of it and Python complement each other perfectly. And last but not least, you can get it for every major operating system.

Once you have Atom and Python installed, let's get right down to business on your first program. I'd recommend firstly that you create a new folder on your computer in an easily accessible place like the desktop or high up on your C drive. Name it something along the lines of Python. I don't recommend adding spaces in the name because it will slow down the process of navigating to it by just a little bit. Anyway, after you do that, you're going to open Atom. Once it's open, you're going to right click on the sidebar and click "Add Project Folder". Then you navigate to the project folder on your computer and select it. Then, you double click the folder in the sidebar in order to make it the active folder, and you right click on the sidebar and select "New File". Then after that, you're going to type hello.py.

In the file, you're going to type the following:

```
print "hello world!\n"
```

Then go ahead and save. Open up your Terminal or Powershell in order to run this. Navigate to the file you just made. If you don't know how to navigate in the command line, it's a worthwhile skill for any programmer in the making. If you don't know how to get around in the command line, then you need to. You can find a lot of useful and simple guides on Google that can teach you the basics in no time. I'm sorry to keep delegating things to Google searches, but it's really just that these topics go far beyond the scope of this book and, in the interest of staying focused and on topic, I think it's pertinent that I stay relevant to the topics at hand.

Anyway, you're going to navigate to the file and run it with the following command:

```
python hello.py
```

If everything goes according to plan, then you should get an output just like this:

```
hello world!
```

If that's the case, then congratulations! You just wrote your very first Python program. You've taken the first crucial steps to being a fully able programmer. It's all uphill from here.

In the next chapter, we're going to be discussing things such as Python math, values, and variables. These may sound boring, but trust me: they're foundational to everything else you'll be doing in this language.

Chapter 2) 7 tips and tricks for a beginner python programmer

You may have experience writing with another programming language such as JavaScript. While that is wonderful, it is not going to assist you when it comes to working with Python really.

Python is a programming language that is going to differ from most other programming languages that you have operated previously if you have not already noticed. One way that it is different from programming languages such as Javascript is that if a data type in Python is empty, it is going to be returned as false, and if it is not empty, it will be returned as true.

Objects and Their Truthfulness

Python is going to check to see if the data type is empty or not, so you are not going to have to check before you place it into your program. For example, if your tuple has a length of zero or it is equal to having inserted an empty tuple, you will have tripped Python's checker to go in and check the truthfulness of the object that you have entered.

With that being said, any number that you place into Python is going to give you a truthfulness of true, but, if you enter zero, you are automatically going to get a false.

In the examples that you are going to see below, a_string is going to be your string because it is one of the types in Python that is going to be checked for truthfulness. You can use strings, tuples, lists, or dicts when you want Python to check for the integrity of the objects that are in them.

Example one:

A_string = project

#this is a true example because the string is not empty

Example two:

A_string = ‘ ‘

#this one is false due to the fact that nothing has been entered into the string actually making it an empty string.

Example three:

If len(a_string) > zero:

Print ‘a_string is not actually empty’

#due to the fact that Python considers zero to be an empty type, then you are going to get a false evaluation of your type when Python checks for the truthfulness of its objects. This is going to occur even though you do not think that it should since zero is a number, but that is not going to matter to Python because it is not how the program was written.

Python Lambda Functions

There are going to be moments in your code that you need to take a function and make it pass as an argument. Or, you may realize that you are required to do an operation that is short but complex several times in a row, and you do not want to type it out as many times as you need it to be repeated.

One option you have is to define your function the normal way, or you can go with the second option which is to create a lambda function that is going to take the expression and return the proper result for how many times you need it to be repeated. No matter which plan you choos, you are going to be defining your function in the exact same way.

Example

Def subtract (c, z): result c – z

Add 3 = lambda c, z: c-z, c-z, c-z

One of the great things that you are going to discover about using the lambda function is that you are going to be using it as an expression and that means that you are going to have the knowledge to place it on a different statement.

With this example, you are going to see the map function calling on functions for every element that is located in the list which is then going to give you a list of results.

Example:

```
square = map (lambda c: c*c, [ 6, 7, 8, 2, 1])
```

Your result is going to be: [36, 49, 64, 4, 1]

If you did not have the lambda function, then you would be forced to define each of your functions separately. With lambda, you will save lines of code as well as variable names for the function that you are using.

The syntax for lambda functions is: lambda variable(s) : expression

Your expression is going to be a Python expression. The scope is always going to include the local scope as well as the variables. The expression is going to be what your function returns.

The variables will be the list that is separated by commas for your variables that the function is going to receive. You are not going to be able to use any keywords or parentheses. If you use parentheses, then your lambda function is not going to work properly.

Using the Map and Filter Functions on Your List at the Same Time

Everyone has their own opinion when it comes to lists in Python. With the list comprehension, you are going to have the ability to use map and filter functions. Some people who use Python believe that these functions are a waste of time. But, you are going to need to make the decision for yourself on if it is worth using or not based on what you are trying to do with Python.

While you have the option of using map and filter separately, you can also use them together as well.

Let's say that you need to see the square root of every number that is under six.

Example

Num = [1, 3, 5, 7, 9]

Squares = [ ]

For num in num:

If num < 6

Squares. Append (num * num)

result: [1, 9, 25]

While you have successfully gotten the answer that you want, your code is starting to get longer, and that is not something that you are wanting to happen, you want your code to be as few lines as you can possibly make it that way if an error code occurs, you are going to have the ability to go through the code quickly in order to figure out where the error might have occurred. This is where the map and filter functions are going to come into play.

Example:

```
Num = [ 1, 3, 5, 7, 9]

Squares = map(lambda a: a*a, filter (lambda a: a < 6, num))

# result [ 1, 9, 25]
```

While the code is smaller, it is not easy to read, and that is not what you want out of the code that you are working with. If you cannot read your code, then what is the point of even using it?

Here, let's now explore what the list comprehension function would make the code look like.

Example:

```
Num = [ 1, 3, 5, 7, 9]

Squares = [ num * num for num in num if num < 6 ]

# result [ 1, 9, 25]
```

Same results and the code is much easier to read. While using the map and filter functions, you are going to get a shorter block of code; it is wiser to use a longer code block so that your script is readable.

As I stated before, you will find those who will use the map and filter functions and others that would rather change their code so that they do not have to use these functions. The choice is going to be yours, but as you can see from the examples listed above, the map and filter function is going to get complicated depending on your code.

The ultimate goal is to make your code as clean as possible, and if using these functions makes it possible, then go for it!

List Comprehension Generator Expressions

List comprehension is great to use, but there is a downside to using it. Not everything is fool proof, and the biggest disadvantage to using list comprehension is that your whole list is going to have to be placed in the memory at the same time. This is not going to be a problem when your list is small and only contains a few objects. However, when your list is rather large, you are only going to be wasting your time.

Using generated expressions is something that came out with Python 2.4 and has changed the number of people who use list comprehension around. When you are using generator expressions, they are not going to load your entire list into the memory bank at once; instead, it is going to create an object that makes it to where only one element that is on the list is loaded at a time.

Should you need to use your entire list for whatever reason, using a generated expression is not really the way to go. However, if you are just trying to pass your expression off for something such as a "for" loop, then the generator function is going to work perfectly.

The syntax for a generator expression is going to be the same syntax that you use when using list comprehensions; the only difference is going to be that your parentheses are going to be on the outside of the brackets.

Example

```
Num = (2, 4, 6, 8)

Squares_under_30 = (num * num for num in num if num * num <
30)
```

any square that is under 30 will now generate an object which is going to cause each value that is successive to be called on.

For square in squares_ under_ 30:

Print square,

result: '2, 16'

While the code is not shorter like we would like it to be, it is going to be more efficient than using the list comprehension function because it is going to load your list into the memory bank one element at a time, therefore, making it to where you do not have to agonize about loading it all in at once.

In the event that you want to use this function for a list that contains more elements in it, you do have the option of using the list comprehension technique, but you should only use this if you are wanting to use your entire list at once.

However, you can use whichever method seems right for you in what you are trying to accomplish. It is recommended that you try and use the generator expressions unless you have some reason not to, but in the end, you are not going to see any real difference in the list comprehension and generator expressions unless the list that you are working with is a large list.

Keep in mind, however, that a generator expression is only going to require a single set of parentheses. Therefore, if you are calling on a function with a generator expression, you are only going to be necessary to insert a single set of parentheses.

Checking Conditions for Elements in a List

There are going to be conditions that have to be met by the items that are on your list, and there will be times that you are going to want to ensure that these elements are meeting those conditions.

Should you be using Python 2.5, then your code will look similar to this:

Example:

```
Num = [ 5, 10, 15, 20, 25, 30]

If [num for num in num if num < 5]:

Print 'two elements that are over five.'

# result: there are at least two items that are over five
```

Should there not be any elements in your list that satisfy your condition, then by default, Python is going to create an empty list and evaluate it as false. But, non-empty lists will be set up and evaluated as true if the condition is met. You do not have to assess every item that is on your list. Instead, you can quit as soon as you find one element that causes your condition to be true.

Python 2.5 has a built-in function known as any, and this function is going to do the same thing that you saw above, only your code is going to be shorter and easier to understand. With the any function, it is programmed to bail and give you a true answer after it locates the first element that satisfies your condition. This function can also be used with a generator expression so that you do not have to evaluate every element on your list and you get your true or false answer back.

Example

```
Num = [5, 10, 15, 20, 25, 30]

If any (num < 5 for num in num):

Output: success!
```

If you absolutely want to, you do have the option of checking for every element that meets your condition, if you are not using Python 2.5, then your code is going to look something like this.

Example

```
Num [ 5, 10, 15, 20, 25, 30]

If len (num) == len([ num for num in num if num < 5]):
```

Output: success!

It is in this example that the list comprehension technique is used to filter and see if there are still as many elements that meet the condition as there were before. It is also checking to see if all of the elements are meeting the condition. Sadly, this is not an efficient way to complete this technique due to the fact that there is truly no need to check every element that is on your list to see if it satisfies the condition that you have put into place. But, if you are not using Python 2.5, this could end up being the only option that you have of checking the elements for your condition.

As you move back to Python 2.5, there is another function that you can use known as the all function. Just like the any function, this function was made to bail once it finds a single element that does not meet the condition, therefore making it to where you are given a false evaluation.

Example

Num = [5, 10, 15, 20, 25, 30]

If all (num < 5 for num in num):

Output: success!

Converting Between a Dict and a List in Python

It is not too complicated to take a dictionary and convert it into a list. When you do this, you are going to get a list with all of the keys which will then enable you to cast that dict into a list. But, it is going to be easier and produce a cleaner code for you to use the .keys() on your dictionary so that you get the list of all of the keys in that dictionary. You can also use the .iterkeys() in order to create an iterator. This is done in the same manner that you are going to call on .values() or .itervalues so that you get a list of the values in your dictionary. It is important to remember that your dict is going to be unordered which will make it seem like the values are not in any order that is meaningful.

In an effort to save both the keys and the values of the dict, you are going to need to take that dict and turn it into a list or iterator that contains two items such as a tuple through the use of the .items() or .iteritems() function.

Example:

Dictionary = {‘b’ : 4 ‘c’ : 6 ‘d’: 8}

Dict_into_list = dict.items()

your dict_into_list will now look like this [(‘b’: 4) (‘c’: 6’), (‘d’: 8)]

Now that you have converted your dict into a list, how do you turn it around and take your list so that it can be converted into a dict? You are going to be taking your two element list or tuple and changing it into a dict.

Example:

Dict = [('b', 4] ['c', 6], ['d', 8]

Dict _into_ list = dict.items()

your dictionary is now going to look like this: { 'b': 4, 'c' : 6, "d' : 8}

While you may be asking yourself why would you ever want to convert a dict into a list or a list into a dict, let's look at the next tip to understand how helpful knowing how to convert them really is.

Python Dictionary Comprehensions

As of this moment, Python does not have any comprehensions built in for dictionaries. So, if you are wanting a dictionary comprehension, you are going to have to write out your own code which is going to produce a piece of code that will give you the results of something that is readable and going to be reasonably similar to a list comprehension.

In order to do this, you are going to use the .iteritems() function which will convert your dict into a list as you learned in the previous chapter. From there you are going to take your list and put it through your generator expression or your list comprehension method before you turn it back into a dict.

Example:

Books = {nonfiction: WorldWarII, fiction: ‘BalladofPiney, music: LifeofBobMarley}

Books_at_library = dict([title, genre of book] for title, genere in of book books.iteritems())

Books_at_library result: {WorldWarII: true, BalladofPiney : true, LifeofBobbyMarley: false}

You have no done “dictionary comprehension!” It is not required that you start and end with a dict if you do not want to. You can always do a list or a tuple if that is what you are wanting to use instead.

The code may seem like it is less readable and straightforward than list comprehension, but it is still going to be better than working with a loop that may never end.

Chapter 3) 7 tips and tricks for an intermediate python programmer

Now we begin with the explanation of a word that we've been using for quite some time. The syntax of a language is basically the grammar of the language. It means to write the language properly. There is no room for error or ambiguity in the syntax of the language because as mentioned computers cannot think on their own. They will do what it is told so it needs to be given the correct instructions. For example, when we are providing the print instructions we cannot write Print or PRINT. It has to be print written in small letters because that is what Python interpreter had been told to learn to understand. Writing it in any other way would just send an error message.

As compared to syntax is the semantics of the language. Semantics are the set of rules that determine the meaning of instructions written in a programming language. While syntax is checked by the interpreter at the time of execution of the program, mistakes in the semantics of the program are usually harder to detect. To avoid semantic mistakes, it is advised to spend time on planning and analysis of the problem before starting to code it. If planned properly, the program will have fewer logical and semantical mistakes and thus the implementation will take much less time.

An example of mistake in the semantics of the language is when we calculate the mean of different numbers. Instead of dividing the sum of numbers with the (total number) if we divide it with (total number)-1 the result would be wrong but the interpreter would not show any errors because it does not understand the semantics of the programs, the programmer has to take care of it.

Now let us take a look at various parts of a Python program. Unlike compiler based languages, an interpreter based language does not need a complete program before it can parse it. It can take a single line of code and interpret it for the computer.

Variables

Variables are central to Python and programming in general. What a variable is, simply put, is a way to store a value. For example, variables can store numbers:

oranges = 7

And they can also store text, known as strings:

message = "How is it going?"

They can store whether something is true or false:

hasARideHome = False

and they can also store decimal numbers, called floats:

bodyTemperature = 98.6

You can modify variables, using math. You'd do this like so:

oranges = oranges + 1# would add 1 to "oranges", making it 8

Point is, variables are a way to store a given value, and they can always change. You can't change between types, though. Well, you can, but we'll get to that in a second. Let's say we had a string variable called "var1" which had the value of "3", and a number variable called "var2" which had the value of 3.

var1 = "3"

var2 = 3

var2 represents the actual numeric value 3, where var1 represents the ASCII character 3. Basically, var1 represents a symbol, where var2 represents a number. So you couldn't add the number 8 to var1, but you could to var2.

var1 += 8# would not work : "3" and 8 can't be added

var2 += 8# would work : 3 + 8 = 11, var2 is now 11

Do you get the gist of what I'm getting at here? So that's the crash course on variables.

Expressions

Do you remember how things can be less than or greater than something else? And evaluating those with the respective relevant signs? Well, those are expressions. And they mean something, right?

Take for example the expression 3 < 7, or "3 is greater than 7". This means something, no? It means 3 is greater than 7, and the expression evaluates to true. This is important, remember that concept of expressions evaluating to be true or false, it's going to come in handy momentarily.

There are a lot of different ways in which you can form mathematical expressions in Python. The key thing to remember is that mathematical expressions are just a way of comparing two values. So for this, there are the expression operators which are intended to help you carry out the comparison of two values: **greater than (>), less than (<), greater than or equal to (>=), less than or equal to (<=), equal to (==)**, and **not equal to (!=).** These are the ones that you need to remember.

So knowing they can evaluate to true or false, let's work with a few examples:

3 == 5# would be false, 3 is not equal to 5

3 != 6# would be true, 3 is not equal to 6

3 >= 3# would be true, 3 is greater than or equal to 3

3 <= 6# would be true, 3 is less than or equal to 6

3 > 7# would be false, 3 is not greater than 7

3 < 2# would be false, 3 is not less than 2

If statements

If statements mark the beginning of a huge part of your programming career: learning about logic. Logic defines and guides every single program you will ever write and it defines even the manner in which programs run. There's all kind of logic going on behind the scenes of a program even if you don't happen to see it, too. So what do if statements do? Well, they have this basic structure:

if (**condition**) is true, {

then execute this code.

}

The condition could be anything that can be true or false. This could mean that the condition could be a raw boolean value, like so:

bananas = True

if bananas { (implicitly says “if bananas is true” without an equation)

then run this code

}

Or it could be an expression, like this:

if 3 > 6 { (the code wouldn’t run, 3 is not greater than 6)

then run this code

}

Or it could even be a method which returns a true or false value. Regardless of what it is exactly, the point is that if statements are structured to evaluate a condition and act in a certain way if it’s true. Here’s how if statements are structured in Python:

if condition:

code here, INDENTED!

So an example of this code would be:

if bodyTemp > 98.6:

print “You have a fever.”

This is what I like to call a **potential conditional.** There’s a **chance** that a chunk of code could be run, given that the condition is met. So if the body temperature were to be **greater** than 98.6, it would print **“you have a fever”**. If the body temperature **weren’t**, nothing would happen. But what if we want something to happen regardless of whether the condition is met? That's what I like to call an **absolute conditional**, and that's where the next part comes in handy: else statements.

Else statements make the perfect comparison to the if statement. The if statement branch of the code will check to see if a condition is true and launch certain code if it isn't. The else statement will be your catch all and safety net in this whole equation: if the condition **isn't** true, then the else statement will launch.

Here's how we'd set up an else statement corresponding to the previous chunk of code:

```
if bodyTemp > 98.6:

print "You have a fever."

else:

print "You don't have a fever."
```

So no matter what happens, the program would either print "You have a fever." or "You don't have a fever." depending upon the necessary conditions at the time. There are applications for both potential conditionals and absolute conditionals and you'll learn those applications as you work with either concept more and get more experience overall in the world of Python programming.

So what if we have multiple conditions that we want to test? This is where else-if statements come in handy. These are conditions that are evaluated after the primary if statement if the primary if statement turns out not to be true, but they are evaluated **before** the else statement so that if the else-if statement is true, the else statement doesn't launch at all. Observe the following code:

```
if bodyTemp > 98.6 and bodyTemp < 102:

print “You have a low fever. Get some rest, you probably are fighting an infection or illness.”

elif bodyTemp >= 102:

print “You have a high fever. Go see a doctor, there could be a serious problem.”

else:

print “You don’t have a fever.”
```

This program will actually evaluate the user's fever and give them an appropriate response. Let's say this user's temperature was 103. Well, the first if statement would look at it and say “well, the body temp is greater than 98.6, but it isn't less than 102. It fails.” and it would send it to the next statement, which checks to see if the temperature is greater than or equal to 102. It would pass this test, so the second condition would be the one which is met and the resultant text would be output to the screen.

Did you notice on the first condition how we evaluated **two** conditions? This is done using something called a conditional operator.

Conditional operators

There are three conditional operators that you need to know: **and**, **or**, and **not**. These all serve their own purposes and function rather similarly. They're used to change the way that an if statement parses the logic of the condition.

The **and** operator checks to see if both conditions are true. So if I had 5 bananas and the condition was like this:

```
if bananas <= 4 and bananas != 1:

# code here
```

Then the condition would be failed, because I have 5 bananas. 5 is not less than or equal to 4. So even though the right side of the condition is correct (5 != 1), the left side is not, and thus the whole thing fails.

The **or** operator, however, just checks to see if either condition is true. So if we took the same scenario and looked at this chunk of code to see how it functioned, we'd see a different outcome:

```
if bananas <= 4 or bananas != 1:

# code here
```

The code would actually evaluate to **true**, because even though the left side of the condition is **not** true (5 <= 4), the right side is indeed true (5 != 1), and only one side needs to be true in the context of the **or** conditional operator.

not is the last one, and it functions a little weirdly, but in a very easy to understand matter. It just inverts the condition and checks to see if it's false and will only execute if the condition turns out to be false. So if I had 5 bananas, and ran into the following if statement:

```
if not bananas <= 4:
```

code here

The code would indeed execute, because the if statement is checking to see if the bananas are NOT less than or equal to four. Do you see what's going on here?

Lists

In both Python and in life, there will be times where you really need to group related information. This is really obvious sometimes. But how do you do it? For example, if you were going to go grocery shopping, you wouldn't cut the piece of paper into tiny strips of paper according to the lines on the page and then try to keep up with all of the little strips. No, that's silly. What you'd do instead is just keep them all on one page of course. It'd be far more efficient to just do that. So why on earth would you create multiple little grocery variables for each and every item on your list? It doesn't make any sense.

So now the question is how exactly do you create what is the equivalent of "one piece of paper" in Python? And the answer is quite simple: with lists.

Lists are really easy to set up, you can either declare them as empty lists, like this:

groceryList = []

Or you can declare them with items, like this:

groceryList = ["apples", "paper towels", "grape juice", "chicken"]

You can add items to the list super easily by using the **append()** method..

groceryList.append("cabbage")

You can reference items from the list by referring to their index location. Python is a programming language, which means it talks to the computer, and computers are weird, so the count actually starts from zero. This means that the first item in the list would be at index location zero. So if we did this:

print groceryList[0]

It would print "apples", which is the first item in the list.

Items can also be really easily removed from lists by way of the del keyword. When you delete an item from a list, everything else will shift back in its place, and it's a really simple way to get rid of items from the list. Let's say we found an old stash of paper towels at home and realized we didn't need them. We'd need to remove the second item from the list, so we'd be removing index position one.

del groceryList[1]

Everything after paper towels in the list would now be shifted back an index position, so that **grape juice** is now at position one rather than position two, chicken is at position two rather than position three, and so on.

Loops

There are two main kinds of loops in Python. Both of them serve different purposes but they also both will be absolutely instrumental to you going forward in Python. These loops are what will make or break you and will absolutely constitute the vast majority of the logic for any given program that you write. Most of the programs that you will ever write will be controlled by a loop in one way or another, and they're simply put the most effective way to introduce logic and control flow into your programming.

The first kind of loop is the while loop. The while loop basically says "hey, I'm going to run for as long as **x condition** is true. When it stops being true, I'll quit running." The basic structure for a while loop in Python is like this:

```
while condition:

# code to run
```

Here's how you would code a loop which counts from 1 to 5 in Python using the while loop.

```
a = 1

while a <= 5:

print a

a += 1
```

What this loop does is say "while the variable **a** is less than or equal to 5, I'm going to print out the value of **a** and then increase **a** by a factor of one."

While loops are really simple to grasp. Their main function comes about when you start to work with game loops. What game loops basically are is a loop which runs while a boolean condition such as **running** or **hasExited** is true. For as long as this variable is true, the program will loop over and over. The variable is made false from within the loop by a given condition, such as the user entering "exit" or pressing "quit" or hitting 0 health. Don't be confused, though, this kind of loop isn't solely reserved for games. Any program which loops over itself for as long as the user has logic to enter will function based on a game loop.

There are also **for** loops. **For** loops are intended for one purpose alone: iteration. For loops in Python are really cool because they actually make iteration through a list or list-type object like File objects super easy for the programmer to work with.

Here's the basic syntax for the Python for loop:

```
for iteratorVariable in iteratedList:

# code goes here
```

Let's take the groceryList list from earlier. If we wanted to loop through it and print off every item on the list, here's the syntax for it:

```
for i in groceryList:

print i
```

It's super simple but, then again, it's not really supposed to be complicated. The preceding code would print out this:

```
apples

grape juice

chicken

cabbage
```

Methods

It's impossible to really write a proper introductory crash course on Python and somehow leave out the all-important notion of methods. Methods are prolific. Methods are important. Methods make up the vast majority of Python code and code in general, and they're what makes it possible for code to be reused and for simple functions like list.**append()** to be possible. It's of the utmost importance that you understand what methods are and how they're applied within the world of programming.

What a method basically is is a chunk of code which can be called from other places within the program as many times as you wish. You can choose to send arguments to the method, if you wish, or you can opt to not send arguments to it. Arguments are basically values that are sent to the method for it to manipulate and change however you'd like for it to do so.

Here's the barest way that methods are structured in C-style languages:

data-type function(arguments) {

code goes here

}

"Data types" aren't expressed in Python methods, though, since Python has implicit data types and not explicit data types. Data types in the context of methods refers to the data type that the method returns. Methods can **return** values, should you want them to, which basically means that they'll give a value **back**. This means that you can actually assign a variable the end result of a function. This is why you can use the raw_input() method to get user input and save the result directly to a variable: when you use the raw_input() method, the user is prompted to enter a string. The raw_input() method returns the **value** of this string, which means that you can save the value it gets back directly to a variable, like so:

```
userInput = raw_input("When is your birthday?")

# if the user entered "May", then the raw_input() method

# would return "May" as its value. userInput would take

# whatever the return value of raw_input() was as its

# own value. The value of userInput would thus be

# "May".

userInput == May

# would print True.
```

So how do we set up a method in Python? It's rather simple, actually, as are most things in Python. This is the structure for methods in Python:

```
def function(arguments):

# code goes here, again INDENTED
```

As an aside, it's imperative that you pay super close attention to Python's indention practices. Other C-style languages don't both too much with indention; they see whitespace as an organizational tool. Python sees whitespace as an organizational tool, as well, but turns that idea on its head a bit. Indentions are thus used in Python mainly for the purposes of denoting hierarchy. Indentations can tell you where a loop begins and ends or where a function starts and ends, and makes invalid the pesky brackets of other C-style languages. It makes Python look far more pragmatic and cleaner, and makes the code itself a lot easier to read at times. There is no good or bad way, here, it's all a stylistic preference, and Python's stylistic preference is that **indentions matter**. SO pay attention there.

So let's say that we wanted to write a method which took an argument of a string to print multiple times, and the number of times to print that string. It would then print the string according to how many times the user specified to print said string. Here's how we'd do it.

First, we'd set up the basic method itself:

def loopString(userString, numberLoops):

Then we'd create a for loop which would loop the number of times that the programmer specified:

for i in range(numberLoops):

the **range()** method creates something for the **for** loop

to iterate through, with as many iteration sequences as

its argument specifies; if the user said numberLoops was 5,

the loop would iterate through range(5), so it would loop 5 times.

Next we just have to write the print statement for the string.

print userString

And voila, you're done. The method ends up looking like this:

```
def loopString(userString, numberLoops):
for i in range(numberLoops):
print userString
```

That makes up the bulk of the heaviest Python topics for you to learn as a beginner, but that doesn't mean there isn't more for you to learn. For example, to be an able Python programmer, you'll really want to learn about things like file input and output and object oriented programming, just two things which are absolutely vital to any able Python programmer's arsenal.

Chapter 4) 7 tips and tricks for an expert python programmer

Before we go on to learning about how to write a function let us first discuss what the benefits of writing a function are. One might argue why we should dissect the program in a disjointed sequence of statements and disturb the flow of execution.

The following is the list of main benefits of writing a function:

- It makes the program more readable and understandable. If we name a group of statements that performs a specific function, we specify their use accordingly in the function name. Now we know whenever we will call the function it will work the same function that we called.

- Functions make the program much smaller. If do not have to write the recitative code again and again. We just write it once in a function and then make the call repetitively.

- If a program is wisely divided into parts, it is much easier to debug it and find errors in it. When we know which part of program does what we just go to that part and update it whenever the need arises.

- If a program is well written and properly debugged it can be saved and then imported to be used in other programs.

The function definition is very important. It should convey the meaning as to what the function does. It should be concise and have proper meaning. For example, if there is a function that calculates the sum of some number, name it sum or calcSum. Another important thing is to decide when to divide a program into a function. Ideally a function is a unit of a program so it is supposed to do a single task. When you a generating a student transcript there should be one function that calculates the grade for individual courses, on that calculates semester GPAs and have another that calculates the cumulative GPAs atleast. Writing a function is a shrewd task and one learns with experience when to divide a program into a function and make it work.

Defining a function

Now let us come to the main part of defining a function. The function definition consists of the name of the function and the arguments it takes as well as the sequence of statements that the function executes. The first line of the function is known as the header and the rest of the function is called the body.

The rules of the function name are the same as those of variable names, only capital and small letters and numbers or underscores. The name cannot begin with a number and avoid using reserved words as a name. Whenever you have used a name for a function, avoid using the same name for a variable.

Here you see the first two print statements have quotes while the last two lines have double quotes. Although single and double quotes can both be used and it is up to us to choose whichever but if there is a single quote or apostrophe within a sentence then we should use double quotes outside.

When the function ends give an empty line. The statements in a function are indented to be grouped together. It is four blank spaces before beginning the line of code. The interpreter will keep on giving an (…) elliptical until it receives an empty line.

When we define a function, a function object is created with the name we have given to it. If we print the object it gives us following information about the function.

```
>>> print print_poem

<function print_poem at 0xb7e99e9c>

>>> print type(print_poem)

<type 'function'>
```

The **type** function is used to know the type of print_poem and as it states it is a type of function object. The empty parenthesis in this function definition indicates that this function takes no arguments. Now let us take a look at a function that takes arguments and returns a value.

General Concepts of Python Coding

Before we get properly into the book, these are the general concepts of coding that you should be aware of; concepts that will make life easier for you.

Explicit Code

While you can do all sorts of weird and wonderful things with Python, it is best to keep it straightforward and explicit.

A Bad Example:

```
def make_complex(*args):
    x, y = args
    return dict(**locals())
```

A Good Example:

```
def make_complex(x, y):
    return {'x': x, 'y': y}
```

Compare these examples; in the latter example of code, we explicitly received x and y from the caller and the return is an explicit dictionary.

The developer who wrote this knows what to do just by looking at the first line and the last line; this is not the case with the bad example.

One Line, One Statement

While there are compound statements, like the list comprehensions, that are allowed and, in many cases, appreciated, it is not good practice to have 2 statements that are disjointed on one code line.

A Bad Example:

```
print 'one'; print 'two'


if x == 1: print 'one'


if <complex comparison> and <other complex comparison>:
    # do something
```

A Good Example:

```
print 'one'
print 'two'


if x == 1:
    print 'one'


cond1 = <complex comparison>
```

```
cond2 = <other complex comparison>
if cond1 and cond2:
   # do something
```

Returning Values

When you get a function that is ever-growing in complexity, it isn't unheard of to use several return statements in the body of the function. However, if you want to maintain clear intent and a good level of readability, you should try not to return values from several points in the function body.

When it comes to returning values within a function, there are 2 cases for doing so: the result that comes from a normally processed function return, and the errors that are indicative of incorrect input parameters or for any reason that the function cannot complete the computation.

If you don't want exceptions raised for the latter case, then it might be necessary for values, such as False or None to be returned, as an indication that the function was not able to perform properly. In cases such as this, it is best practice to return as soon as the wrong context has been noticed.

This will help to neaten up the function structure because all code that comes after the error return assumes that the condition has been met so that the main function result can be computed. As such, it is sometimes necessary to have several return statements like this.

That said, if a function contains several different courses it can go, it can be unwieldy to debug the result so it is preferable to maintain just one course. This also helps in working out code paths and, if you have several courses, it could be an indication that you need to re-look at your code and tidy it up.

Programming Recommendations

These are the basic recommendations for writing Python code, recommendations that you should follow if your code is going to be more effective and efficient as well as being readable.

Your code must be written so that it doesn't disadvantage other Python implementations, such as IronPython, Jython, PyPy, Psyco and Cython.

For example, you should never rely on the efficient string concatenation of CPython that takes the form of ***a=a+b*** or ***a+=b.*** This is a somewhat fragile optimization, even though it super-efficient in CPython, because it won't work on al type sand it won't be present in any Python implementation that does not use refcounting.

Instead, where you use a part of the library that is performance-sensitive, you should use the ***.join()*** form instead. This will make sure that the concatenation is linear across all the different Python implementations.

Never use an equality operator to make comparisons to a singleton such as None. Instead, use ***is*** or ***not.***

You should also be wary of using **if x** when really you should be using **if is not None**. An example of this is when you are testing if an argument or a variable that defaults to a value of None was actually set to a different value. The other value could have a type that is false in the Boolean context.

Rather than using the operator **not…is**, you should use **is not**. While they both are identical in terms of function, the first is low on the readability scale, making the second one more preferable. An example:

Use This:

if foo is not None:

Don't Use This:

if not foo is None

When you implement an ordering operation with a rich comparison, you should implement all of the 6 operations instead of relying on some other code to exercise a comparison. Those operations are ***(__eq__, __lt__, __ne__, __ge__, __gt__, __le__)***

To cut down on the effort needed, one particular decorator helps to generate any comparison methods that are missing. That decorator is ***functools.total_ordering().***

The style guidelines indicate that Python assumes reflexivity rules. As such, the Python interpreter might change things about by swapping ***y > x*** with ***x < y*** , or it may swap ***y >= x*** with ***x <= y*** .

You may also find that the argument ***x == y*** has been swapped with ***x != y*** . The ***min()*** and ***sort()*** operations will also definitely use the < operator and the ***max()*** function will use the >operator. However, you should, as a best practice guide, use all of them so that there is no confusion.

Rather than using an assignment statement that will bind a lambda expression to an identifier, use a ***def*** statement

A Good Example:

```
def f(x): return 2*x
```

A Bad Example:

```
f = lambda x: 2*x
```

The first example shows that the name given to the function object is ‘f’ rather than the collective <lambda>. This is the most useful for string representations and for tracebacks and, by using the assignment statement, you cut out the one benefit that a lambda expression offers over and above a def statement – that it may be embedded within a bigger statement.

When you want to derive exceptions, use Exception and not BaseException. Inheritance from the latter is reserved for those exceptions where it is pretty much always wrong to catch them

When you design your exception hierarchies, base them on the quality that is likely to be needed by catching exceptions, rather than on the location where the exception is raised. Always answer one question – “what has gone wrong?” rather than just saying that something is wrong. Use the conventions for class naming but do remember to add the “Error” suffix to the exception classes that produce an error.

There is no need to put any special suffixes on exceptions that are not errors and are used as flow-control or another form of signaling.

When you use exception chaining, use it only where needed.

When you replace an inner exception deliberately, make sure that the right details are relocated into the newer exception. Examples of this are making sure the name of the attribute is preserved when you convert ***KeyError*** to ***Attribute Error*** or when you embed the original exception text into the message in the newer exception

When using Python 2 and you raise an exception, always use the ***raise ValueError)'message')*** instead of ***raise ValueError 'message'***

This is because the second example is neither valid nor legal syntax for Python 3. Also, the use of the containing parentheses means that there is no requirement to use continuation characters on a line when you add string formatting or when an exception argument is too long.

When you catch exceptions, always mention specific ones wherever you can rather than using the bare except: clause

This is the ONLY syntax that Python 3 supports and it cuts out any problems of ambiguity that are associated with the older-style syntax that is comma-based.

When you are catching system errors, use the exception hierarchy from Python 3.3 rather than errno values. As well, when you use any try/except clause, try to limit the use of the try clause to the least amount of code. This will cut down the risk of errors being hidden

When you use a resource tool that is local to a specific code section, use it with a statement to make sure that it is cleaned immediately after use. You can also use a try/finally statement

Always invoke a context manager through separate methods or functions whenever they are for a purpose other than getting and releasing resources.

The second example does not give us any information that indicates whether the __enter__ and __exit__ methods do anything other than shutting the transaction. In this case, it is important to be explicit.

Consistency in return statements is important. Either all of the function return statements or none of the return statements should return an expression or value. If a return statement does return an expression, any that do not return any value should state explicitly that the return is None and there should be a return statement at the end of that function

Don't use string modules; use string methods instead

These are always faster and they share an API with the Unicode strings. This rule can be ignored if you need backward compatibility with a Python implementation that is earlier than 2.0

Instead of using string slicing as a way of checking for suffixes and prefixes, use ***".startswith()*** and ***".endswith()*** instead

These are much cleaner methods and they are less prone to errors.

When you check to see if an object is actually a string, remember that it could be a Unicode string as well. In Python 2.0, Unicode and str share the base class called ***basestring*** so you could do:

```
if isinstance(obj, basestring):
```

However, in Python 3, you won't find basestring or Unicode, only str and bytes objects are not strings anymore, they are integer sequences instead.

Don't include any string literals that require significant levels of trailing whitespace because this is not distinguishable and some text editors will remove them

Don't use == to compare a Boolean value to True or False:

A Good Example:

if greeting:

A Bad Example:

if the greeting == True:

An Even Worse Example:

if the greeting is True:

Code Layout

The most obvious place to start with is how to layout your code. I will be giving you the best practice guidelines for code layout along with examples on how to do it and how not to:

Indentation and Alignment

Every indent level should be 4 spaces.

When you use continuation lines, they should align the wrapped elements using one of two methods:

Vertically with the Python implicit way of joining lines inside braces, brackets, and parentheses, or

With hanging indents

When you use a hanging indent, consider that there shouldn't be any arguments on line one and that, to mark the continuation line, indentation must be used.

When you use an if-statement with a long condition that can be written over more than one line, note that there is an easy to create a natural indent of 4 spaces for the rest of the lines in the conditional – use a keyword of 2 characters (for example, if) along with one space and an opening parenthesis. However, visually, this can look like some kind of incompatibility with the indented code within the if-statement, which will already have a 4-space indent. There is no real position on whether to distinguish these conditional lines from the code inside the nest but there are a few acceptable options you can use, including but not limited to:

Now, when you have a construction of multiple lines, the closing brace, parentheses, or bracket can line up in one of two places – either beneath the beginning character that is NOT a white space on the end line of the list:

```
my_list = [
    6, 5, 4,
    3, 2, 1,
```

```
    ]
result = a_function_that_will_take_arguments(
    'f', 'e', 'd',
    'c', 'b', 'a',
    )
```

Or it can be lined up beneath the beginning character of the first line in the multiple line construction:

```
my_list = [
    6, 5, 4,
    3, 2, 1,
]
result = a_function_that_will_take_arguments(
    'f', 'e', 'd',
    'c', 'b', 'a',
)
```

Idioms

Programming idioms are, in simple terms, the way in which Python code should be written. We often refer to idiomatic code as Pythonic code and, although there tends to be one very obvious way to write something, the actual way in which Pythonic code is written can be a bit obscure to those who are new to Python. So, you need to learn good idioms and some of the more common ones are:

Unpacking

Provided you know how long a tuple or list is, unpacking allows you to give each element a name. For example, **enumerate()** gives us a tuple with 2 elements for each of the items in the list:

```
for the index, each item in enumerate(this_list):
    # do something with the index and each item
```

You can also use unpacking to swap the variables:

```
b, a = a, b
```

And you can use nested unpacking:

```
c, (b, a) = 3, (2, 1)
```

When Python 3 was implemented, it came with a new extended unpacking method:

```
c *the_rest = [3, 2, 1]

# c = 3, the_rest = [2, 1]

c, *the_middle, c = [4, 3, 2, 1]

# c = 4, the_middle = [3, 2], c = 1
```

Creating Ignored Variables

If you wanted to assign something but do not need to use the variable, you would use __.

NOTE

You will often see it recommended that you use a single underscore (_) for variables that are throwaway, rather than using a double underscore(__). The problem with this is, "-", the single underscore, tends to be used in the **gettext()** function as an alias. It is also used to store the value of the previous operation at the interactive prompt. When you use a double underscore, "__", it is clear and it is convenient. It also cuts out the accidental risk of interfering with the other use cases of the single underscore.

Creating Length-N Lists

To create a length-N list that is of the same thing, you would use the * list operator

```
four_zeros = [Zero] * 4
```

To create a length-N list of a list you should not use the * operator. That operator creates lists of N that refer to the same list and that is not what we want here.

Searching a Collection for an Item

On occasion, you will need to search a collection for a specific option and there are two ways to do this – using lists or sets

Now, both of these functions look exactly the same simply because **lookup_set** uses that fact that Python sets are hash tables. However, the performance of **lookup** in each of the examples is different. In order to decide whether a specific item is contained in a list, Python has to search through every single item until it finds one that matches. This takes time, especially if you have a long list. With sets, each item has a hash that tells Python where to look for the matching item. This makes the search much quicker even if the sets are big ones. You can also search dictionaries in the same way. Because there is a difference in the performance, it is a better idea to use a set or a dictionary rather than a list in the following cases:

Where a collection contains a lot of items

Where you are going to be searching for items in a collection on a repeated basis

There are no duplicate items

In cases of smaller collections or those that you are not likely to be searching on a frequent basis, the extra memory and time needed to set the hash table up will, more often than not, be more than the time you save by improving the speed of the search

Comments

Because you already have some experience of Python coding, you will know that a comment is invisible when the program is run. A comment is there to help the coder and others who read it to understand what has been done and why. Now, some people think that, because they are invisible then there is no need to write them while others write comments that make no sense and that contradict their code. I have to tell you that, out of the two, having a contradictory comment is far worse than not writing one at all and, as such, whenever you make changes to your code, you must make sure that you update your comments.

When you write a comment, ensure that it is a proper sentence with a proper ending. As it is when you write anything, your comment, be it a sentence or a phrase, must have a capital letter to start it. The only exception to that rule is if it is an identifier that starts with a lower-case letter – a golden rule here is that you NEVER change the case of an identifier!

If you are using a short comment you can leave off the full-stop at the end. If you are writing block comments, these tend to be made up of at least one paragraph, sometimes more, each one built from whole sentences. Each of these sentences must have a full-stop. Following each full-stop there should be 2 spaces and all comments should be written in English. The only exception to this is if you are 200% certain that your code is never going to be read by people who do not speak or read your language

Block Comments:

A block comment tends to apply to some or all of the code that comes after it. The comment should be indented in the exact same way as the code it refers to and each line of each block must begin with a # and one space. The only exception is if you have used indented text within the comment. All paragraphs in each block comment must be separated with a line that contains one #.

Inline Comments

These should be used as little as possible. As a refresher, an inline comment is a comment that is placed on the same line that a statement is on. An inline comment has to be separated from the statement by a minimum of two spaces and they must begin with one # and one space.

In all honesty, you should avoid using inline comments because they are not really necessary and can cause an unwanted distraction.

For example, you should never do this:

```
x = x + 1             # Increment x
```

However, sometimes, this could be useful:

```
x = x + 1             # Compensate for the border
```

Conventions

To make your Python code much read better, follow these conventions:

Look to see if your variables are equal to a constant. There is no need for an explicit comparison of the values to 0, None or True; instead, you could add it into the if-statement.

How to Access Dictionary Elements:

Instead of using the method dict.has-key(), use the syntax, x in d or use dict.get() to pass default arguments to.

Manipulate Lists the Short Way

You don't need to be long-winded when it comes to manipulating lists; use list comprehensions or the filter() or map() functions to use concise syntax when you want to perform an operation on a list.

This function reads better than trying to manually handle a counter and it is far more optimal for iterators

Reading from a File

When you want to read from a file, it is best to use the with open syntax as this will close the files for you automatically.

Using the with statement is far more efficient because it makes sure the file is always closed even when the with block contains an exception

Line Continuations

There are accepted limits to logical code lines and when you have one that is longer, it should be split up over several lines. Your Python interpreter will take consecutive lines and, so long as the final character on each line is a backslash (/), it will join the lines. However, although this can be useful sometimes, really you should avoid doing it because it can be fragile. If you were to add a whitespace after the backslash, it can break your code and the results might not be what you expected.

A better way to do this is to enclose elements inside parentheses. If there is an unclosed parenthesis at the end of the line, the next line will be joined, and so on until there is a closed parenthesis. You could also use square or curly braces to do the same thing, so long as you remain consistent – whatever you use to start, you must also use to finish.

That said, if you find that you are having to keep on splitting up long lines, it is just a sign that you are trying to do too much and this will affect the readability of the code

Method and Function Arguments

For the first argument in any instance method always use self and, for the first argument in any class method, always use cls.

If the name of a function's argument is the same as one of the reserved keywords, then it is best to add one trailing underscore than it is to use a corrupted spelling or an abbreviation. As such, you should ***class_*** rather than ***clss.*** Perhaps even better than causing a clash - use a synonym.

Function Arguments

There are 4 ways that you can pass an argument to a function:

Positional Argument – these are mandatory and do not contain any default values. The positional is the simplest argument form and are used for the arguments that are a complete part of the meaning of a function; they also have a natural order so, in the following example, the function user should find it easy to remember that the 2 functions need 2 arguments and they should remember the order:

Send(message, recipient) and point(x, y)

In both cases, you can use the argument names when you call the functions and, by doing this, you can change the order the arguments are in. However, as you can see from this, it is not very readable and there are way more words there than we need.

Keyword Argument – these do contain default values and they are not mandatory. Keyword arguments are sometimes used for optional parameters that you send to the function. When a function contains at least 2 or 3, preferably more, positional parameters, it is not easy to remember. Using a keyword argument that has a default value is more helpful.

However, you should use the same level of caution that you did with arbitrary argument lists, for pretty much the same reasons. These are powerful techniques that should only be used when you can prove that it is necessary to use them. They most definitely should not be used if there is a clearer and simpler construct that will do the job.

It really is down to you, the programmer, to decide which of the function arguments are optional keywords and which are positional and to determine whether you should use the more advanced techniques to pass the arguments.

Keep it simple and follow these rules of writing Python functions that:

Are readable – the names and the arguments do not need any explanations

Are easily changeable – you can add a keyword argument in without the rest of the code breaking.

Chapter 5) QnA

Chapter 2: Quiz

1. What is computer programming?

2. What is a programming language?

3. What is coding the algorithm.

4. What is Binary code or machine code?

5. What is machine code?

Answers

1. A process of planning and developing a sequence of steps for the computer

2. A set of rules, symbols and special words used to construct a program

3. Translating an algorithm into a programming language

4. It is a combination of 0's and 1's that represent instructions.

5. A program written in high level language is called source code while a program written in binary

Chapter 3: Quiz

1. What is Variable?

2. What is a Value?

3. What is variable type?

4. What is an expression?

5. What is concatenation?

6. What is are comments?

Answers

1. It is a name or label given to a vale so that a program can remember it for later use.

2. It is a name or label given to a vale so that a program can remember it for later use.

3. A category of values

4. It is a combination of variables, values and operators that will amount to a single result.

5. It is joining of two string values together.

Chapter 4: Quiz

1. What is a function?

2. What is an argument?

3. What is a return value?

4. What is a function call

5. What is a deterministic algorithm while the one that does not give the same result is known as non-deterministic.

6. What is flow of execution?

Answers

1. It is named sequence of statements that perform a specific task.
2. It is a value that is passed to the function as an input. A function may have zero, one or more arguments.
3. It is an output that is generated through the function
4. It is a statement that executes a function. It consists of the name of a function and its argument list.
5. Some program or algorithm that gives the same result every time we give the same input is known as deterministic algorithm while the one that does not give the same result
6. It is the order in which the statements in the program run.

Conclusion

The next step is to go beyond this book. I've given you a lot of tools and tricks within this book, some of them very concrete and some of them very abstract, some of them full-fledged lessons and some of them just scraping the very essence of the topic, but it doesn't matter what level of detail I went into if you don't use the information I've given you. I can give you all the tips in the world but if you aren't proactive about using them, then you won't be very good at it.

Programming is a lot like language learning. You can be a very solid speaker of a language by acting minimally, sure. But it's only by devoting yourself to a language and immersing yourself in it that you'll be able to be hang with the best in terms of your ability to speak that language.

Programming is no different. If you aren't proactive, if you don't get involved in online and real life communities and try your best to program as much as you can in as many new ways as you can find, then you're going to plateau, and you're going to plateau very, very hard. I've given you tips and tricks to prevent you from doing exactly this, and if you push yourself and keep going with it, then you'll be on the road to being the best Python programmer that you can absolutely be.

In other words, you will get exactly what you give when it comes to Python. If you give a lot of effort to it and work very hard towards becoming a better programmer, you'll become a better programmer. But this isn't going to happen without direct action by you.

I sincerely hope that this book has helped you to find your voice with Python and find a few solutions to help you progress within the language itself. Maybe it helped you find a way to connect to other programmers, and maybe it helped you realize some of the sheer utility of the list and string objects. Maybe I sparked your interest to start programming video games. Regardless of what I did, at the end of the day, what I hope more than anything is that I've written a book which will help you to be the absolute best programmer that you can be and progress upwards constantly in your journey to be a better Python programmer.

CPSIA information can be obtained
at www.ICGtesting.com
Printed in the USA
LVHW052059270321
682703LV00012B/149